The Stars Are Falling

Reasons To Believe We Are Enslaved By The Serpent

Matthew Delooze

A
Matthew Delooze
Publication

ISBN 978-0-9556296-2-4

Published by Matthew Delooze

www.matthewdelooze.co.uk

www.matthew-delooze.blogspot.com/

First edition 2007

Title previously published by Experiences eBooks 2006

The sun be darkened,
and the moon shall not give her
light,
and the stars shall fall from the
sky,
and the powers of the heavens
shall be shaken.

Matt 24:29

For
'The Rain'

Contents

Introduction.

I am now 48 years old. In 1998/99 I went through a traumatic spiritual awakening. Some people will see this awakening as some kind of nervous breakdown or mental illness. That's fine. I probably would have thought the same thing myself about someone in a similar position before my awakening occurred. After my awakening I regained conscious memories of some strange events that took place throughout my childhood and I also gained direction from a powerful spiritual force that has literally sent me on a journey of truth.

I have waited a long time to write this book. I have also thought long and hard before attempting to provide the information that I wish to pass on to you through the pages ahead of us.

I know in my heart that some people out there desperately need to read the information that I am attempting to supply. I wrote a short book called 'You Will Be Wiser When You're Older' last year. In that book I explained about some of my early childhood experiences regarding abduction and interaction with, what I can only describe as, beings that are alien to this world.

The information I provide in this book is entirely because of my experiences, from childhood, with inter-dimensional beings. Without these experiences, and the spiritual direction that I followed because of them, I could never have written this book.

Thank you

Matthew Delooze

Chapter One
The Long and Dusty Road to Dendera

"Oh, I'm never gonna be the same again,
Now I've seen the way it's got to end,
Sweet dream, sweet dream.
Strange magic"

The lyrics are taken from the song 'Strange Magic' by ELO

I have had strong spiritual forces directing me for several years now. Since 1999 these directional forces have grown in strength and I have far more inner understanding because of them. I am learning more and more each day on how to master the full benefit of my new found direction.

Late 2004 and early 2005 I had very strong urges to visit Egypt. Although short of money it became obvious to me that, no matter what, I just had to go. Somehow, more by luck than management, I managed to arrange the trip which included some very good visits to the ancient Egyptian temples accompanied by an *expert* guide. I also had a lot of free time to study interesting areas myself.

I had heard that the tourist trap in Egypt was to rush you away from the ancient sites as soon as possible after the official guide had finished his usual tourist chatter.

The lesson provided by the official guide whilst visiting the temples was always based on the establishment's version of the historical events linked to the temples and, of course, the official reasons for the temples existing in the first place.

It is fact that the western world has indeed created the official version of ancient Egyptian history anyway and modern day Egyptians haven't got a clue about the origins of their own country apart from what western historians taught them. Anyway, whilst touring the temples, tourists received some basic information from the official guides and as soon as the tour was over they were rushed away to the nearest alabaster gift shop, or papyrus showroom, and vigorously badgered into buying *genuine* assorted alabaster gifts or painted art on papyrus. The punters were literally dragged into the shop and pestered to purchase crappy tourist junk. This 'temple to cash register' policy was no co-incidence either because the guides were on very good commission from the shops owners.

It soon became obvious to me that the educated expert guide tried to sell the gift shop version of Egyptian history during our visits around the ancient temples, and the official guided tours are entirely based on 'temple to cash register' mentality. This situation turned out to be true in certain areas of Egypt but fortunately for me, not in the areas that I was spiritually directed to see. One of those areas was the Temple of Hathor at Dendera.

I was told by a psychic in 1995/6 that I would visit Egypt in the *future*. I am a working class lad and at the time I was slaving away in a factory with a wife and two children to support. I thought the psychic had got me mixed up with somebody else. How would I ever get to visit the ancient temples of Egypt I thought at the time? I couldn't even afford a two bob fluffy camel from the toy shop never mind get to visit places like Abu Simbel and the Great Pyramid at Giza.

I had never even been abroad before the psychic informed me of my fate, apart from one weekend in Amsterdam in 1990, so the claims were a little hard for me to believe at the time because trips like that were not for the likes of me. Up until 1999 I had absolutely no interest in Egypt or ancient temples anyway. I had also no interest or insight in the symbolism surrounding ancient Egypt either.

That said in May 2005 I had the tickets to go to Egypt in my hand and the comments that had previously been made by the psychic came rushing back to me, flooding my memory. I was gob-smacked. How had this psychic known this information?

Everything the psychic had told me in 1995/96 was coming true. I knew I was going to Egypt to learn something important, I just didn't know what.

The psychic had informed me of many other things that had already come true in the build up of events that had led me to Egypt. Can you comprehend the feeling of anticipation I was feeling at the time? What was I going to find out? The time was fast approaching for the start of my trip in late June 2005 but, surprisingly, instead of collecting information about ancient Egyptian history I only checked up on the price and availability of beer and some local customs. Obviously the official history of Egypt wasn't going to help me. Whatever I was going to learn in Egypt, I knew it was not going to come out of a history book or the educated mouth of a so-called Egyptologist. I was going to receive first hand education through my own intuition and spiritual guidance.

My path to Egypt, by this I mean my life experiences up to that time, had been very difficult. Since 1998 I had started to remember things and gain access to the spiritual knowledge inside me that I had literally been blocked from assessing before that time. I believe some kind of access *blocking* procedure had taken place by using complicated mind control techniques, hypnosis if you like, and this was carried out by extraterrestrials/inter-dimensional beings during the early stages of my incarnation in this world. My spiritual abilities had been reduced and basically my limits of awareness had been interfered with.

I ask you, yes you, if it is possible that unseen forces could have also interfered with your access to **your** memories or natural intuition? Could some unknown force managed to gain access to your deepest spiritual awareness? Have you ever thought this to be the case? I now ***know*** my very life-force was tampered with. I always had a little spark in me that knew something had happened to me and that something was not quite right with this world. Do you have the same feeling?

That little spark can never be destroyed no matter what mind control or drugs are used against you. No matter what shit is thrown against you in this world that spark can never die. It will never do so either.

Have you ever had similar ideas or even just a niggling little thing chipping away at the back of your mind trying to get out? Is it possible that your own inner memories and intuition may have been tampered with as well? Is this sort of scenario so difficult to be considered as true? Do you continuously shrug things like this off?

Have you ever really considered that you could also have been somehow blocked from using your spiritual instincts or at least blocked from using them to their full potential? Obviously you would have no proper conscious knowledge of this happening if you if you were suffering from hypnosis or under the control of some other form of mind control. It is so easy to ignore feelings or thoughts that interfere with our five sense reality isn't it?

Only a very slight, niggling and recurring, suspicion may be in your conscious memory at this time but you may just shrug the suspicions off. Don't worry if you harbour such feelings because I had similar feelings to this for 30 years without fully realising what they were about. Then I had a fast track awakening in 1999 and things started to become instantly clearer.

I suppose the best way of explaining this is to mention the movie starring Arnold Schwartzenegger. 'Total Recall'. Have you seen it?

Schwartzenegger plays the part of a man who has had his mind altered and replaced with a false memory. A new life has been created for him and he cannot access his real memory. He lives out his created life totally unaware that he is living with a manufactured memory. Even his personality has been changed to fit in with the new life that was created for him by unseen powers that did not want him to remember his true self or his old life. The situation drastically changes when he suffers from traumatic shock and the distress causes his mind to slowly reject the false memory that was placed in him. He starts to remember incidents from his previous life that he couldn't previously recall. A mixture of mind control and drugs had kept him totally oblivious of the true situation surrounding his past life and the fact that his new life was totally controlled.

Eventually he manages to obtain total recall of his true life and situation because of the effect of the trauma he suffered. He eventually saw through the lies that had kept his manufactured life together. The deception fell   apart because of his curiosity and questioning and he eventually realised that his life was really an empty sham based on hypnotism. It was only after he fully realised that he had been duped on a massive scale that his manufactured world collapsed all around him and was exposed for what it really was, a controlled Illusion.

The original covers for Total Recall ©Tri-Star Pictures, starring Schwarzenneger. Please note the eye and pyramid symbolism and I also ask you 'How would you know if someone stole your mind?

The same scenario applies to the whole of mankind today. We are each living a sham of a life and have done so over and over again for thousands of years. You have lived numerous lives in a hypnotic trance without realising that you are a spiritual prisoner and a slave. You are existing under the complete control of multidimensional alien beings.

It's hard to accept I know! Anyway, let us move on.

Do you have some inexplicable feelings inside you and somehow you just know things are not as they should be in this world?

I certainly did for most of my life, but such thoughts were soon abandoned without mercy, simply because of the constant pressure from everyday living and thoughts about our *reality*. Such thoughts as earning a living, trying to make ends meet, caring for children, fitting in with fashions, money and politics etc. These five sense thoughts literally rule the roost and take priority over any other thoughts especially ones about the possibility that we may be living a big lie in this chicken shack that our world has become. Our minds are constantly forced to think on how to survive.

We spend so much time trying to survive that we don't know why we want to survive in the first place.

I call this world a 'chicken shack' because this planet has simply become a building full of spiritual cowards. I may sound harsh but aren't fearful people who have no spirit or courage described as being *chickens*? Yes?

Then that is how I see this world in 2006, a Chicken Shack. When I look back on my life I can remember events when I chickened out of doing the right thing. I am sure you can too. Even from an early age something inside me made me look for and always take the easy option. The older I got the easier it became. Where did this selfish 'I'm alright Jack' attitude come from?

I remember several school chums having to take punishment for my crimes so to speak. For example, on one occasion I accidentally squirted blue ink down the back of my teacher's white blouse and pink skirt, as she wandered round the classroom. I really didn't mean to do it, the pen was faulty and the only action that made the pen work was swaying it through the air in a downward motion until ink was forced through the nib. Unfortunately for me, I did this too vigorously and the ink silently hit the back of the teachers clothes, splatting her with dark blue ink. I was gob- smacked but luckily she never noticed and, even luckier, she was on her way back to her desk. All the other kids had their heads down working and they hadn't seen my silent weapon hit the teacher. I immediately got my head down too and started writing. The teacher then sat at her desk and she was facing the class. Nobody could see the line of ink that ran down her back.

The lesson ended, it was break time and we went out for play in the school yard. On returning to the classroom, after *playtime,* we were met with a red faced 'Miss'. She was bloody fuming. "Who has done this to my skirt and blouse?" she said. There was utter silence. You could have heard a pin drop. The teacher raged, "If no one owns up to doing this damage to my skirt and blouse I will punish all the class". I expected somebody, anybody, that had actually witnessed events to look at me with some sort of a; "Go on Matthew give yourself up" look, but nobody did and it became obvious that there were no eye witnesses to my crime. I smiled to myself.

I felt compelled to admit my sin but something came over me and I kept very quiet. I really didn't want sending to the headmistress, higher authority, to be punished for my accidental crime. I knew the headmistress could deal out harsher punishment and really hurt me. The teacher tried and tried to get a confession out of somebody in class but she failed to get even a murmur from my classmates. In her frustration the whole class was punished by being made to sit in silence for the lesson (one hour) with their hands on their head. I felt really guilty about this.

Why had I not had the guts to admit it was me? What made me allow all the class to be punished for my sin? I chose to do the right thing for me, and not just do the right thing. Yet I still got punished didn't I? I could have saved a lot of people from injustice simply by telling the truth but I was too scared to tell the truth because of the embarrassment it would cause me personally. I somehow knew that I would not be believed should I have claimed it was all an accident. I also suppose it was far easier to see others receive the same punishment as me than face the punishment all on my own. The same scenario has happened over and over again throughout my life at work and at play.

What made me do 'not the right thing'? What made me do the right thing for me instead of just doing the right thing full stop or the right thing period?

Is it natural for humans to behave like this? Or is it just that the average human is so easily led or simply fearful about the system we live under?

Do we accept our own oppression simply because we see or hear about other people who are more oppressed than ourselves? My experience with the ink and my teacher, all those years ago in class, certainly indicates to me that we do. We seem to take oppression for granted as long as others are also oppressed. Is it a case that we go along with a corrupt system simply because more fearful systems with even higher levels of corruption exist elsewhere?

"Our oppression is not as bad as oppression in the third world" I hear people say. I say, with respect to George Orwell, "We are all equally oppressed but some are more equally oppressed than others". Let me say that the *same* forces cause oppression all over the world. They decide how much force is used and in which area of the globe it is located. The same forces also decide the particular time and location to increase oppression. What is happening in Africa today can be made to happen anywhere else on the planet tomorrow, anywhere at all. Just what has happened to human emotions in this world?

I find that acts of human kindness are very rare, so rare in fact that they really do stand out when they are seen to happen or do actually happen to you. Why is this?

Why do animals seem to have strong instincts and a sort of natural spiritual awareness that we humans cannot match? Animals can sense many things that humans can't. Why is this? My own ego prior to 1999 would have insisted that I was more spiritually intelligent than, say, the average otter or a duck billed platypus. Indeed prior to 1999 I would have laughed at anyone who suggested that a golden hamster had more spiritual intuition than me? Sadly this is not the case now. I now **know** my spiritual intuition was sabotaged for many years. I had never knowingly followed my intuition prior to 1999, I only followed my education. I now know that my intuition had literally been taken away from me. It had been stolen.

Is it possible that we have all been blocked from using our in-built spiritual abilities? Do we follow what we are taught and not what we really feel?

Are these abilities really vital to us to assist us to adhere to a pre-arranged spiritual life plan whilst in this world and will our true spiritual intent fail without these abilities?

I think so yes. Yes it will, and it has for many of our lifetimes.

Have we been taught how to think? How to behave? Have we been trained to achieve an official *I'm Alright Jack* award and have an *I'm Alright Jack* badge placed over our hearts? We automatically follow our educational teachings and we totally ignore our natural awareness, don't we? In other words we are made to abandon our intuition and we are bribed into obeying education and religious teachings. We robotically follow the footsteps of fools and deceivers that have ruined this world, instead of trusting ourselves.

My intuition made me go to Egypt in 2005 and not false education or dogmatic religion. I simply followed 'me'. I would never have taken the dusty road to Dendera without following my full and proper instinct or intuition and it would have been impossible to do so if I had only followed my educated mind.

I am so glad I followed my intuition.

....

Chapter two
A Chicken Shack Controlled By the Crocodiles.

"What the masses think they get - they get."
Matthew Delooze 2004.

In five sense reality terms I believe that a race of extraterrestrials /
multidimensional beings covertly rules this planet. These extraterrestrials
can flit from dimension to dimension (world to world) and can actually
snatch people from this dimension, either physically or mentally and take
them to another dimension. I believe these extraterrestrials are reptilian
in shape and nature. This sounds bloody daft I know but I suppose the
giraffe thinks that humans look silly too! I call this group of beings the
Serpent Cult and this 'Serpent Cult' have controlled the physical reality
and spiritual destiny of mankind for thousands of years. When I mention
the words 'Serpent Cult' I maybe referring to their human agents on
Earth.

Meanings of the word 'cult'.

> The English word *cult* comes from the French *word*
> *culte*, which came from the Latin word *cultus*
> (care and adoration), which came from the Latin
> word *colere* (to cultivate).
> There is no generally accepted, single current
> definition for the word *cult*, or for many other
> religious terms. This leads to confusion over the
> meanings of certain religious terms. A reader
> must often look at the context in which the word
> is used in order to guess at the intent of the writer.

The Serpent Cult harnesses our spiritual power and they somehow
feed off it and use it against us. They do this by creating our physical
reality through collective mind control. To control our reality they need
to control our thoughts. If they control our thoughts then they also
control our actions.

This is true, they not only control your physical life here on this planet, the planet you call Earth, they also control your thoughts, therefore your soul, when you leave the physical body. They shout physical shit and we jump on the physical shovel. They shout spiritual shit and we jump on the spiritual shovel. Your reality is being controlled both in and out of your physical body. Death at this present moment in time on this planet is no escape from the control the Serpent holds over you. They click their fingers and we are immediately placed in a hypnotic trance and we are rendered instantly heartless or immediately become fearful. 'Puppets'.

Just look at the Iraq situation and ask yourself how that came about if we live in a free world. Despite the fact that the invasion was illegal and immoral it still went ahead and indeed we still occupy Iraq. This is a prime example of chicken shack control. The owners of a chicken shack can march into it and strangle as many chickens as they want. The rest of the chickens will do absolutely nothing about it and sadly, they will still sit there producing eggs for the rulers the shack.

The rulers of our world, our chicken shack, are the Serpent Cult.

When the Serpent Cult controls our thoughts they can easily rule our world. If they stop controlling our thoughts then our natural intuition, our spiritual awareness, would simply return. We would become natural again, spiritually free, instead of the spiritual prisoners we are now.

I will write about the chicken shack in the form of a parable. To understand the parable the way I mean it, I will say that by using the term chicken shack I mean the planet Earth and when I use the term crocodiles I am referring to the inter-dimensional forces that surround planet Earth and control us. We, the human race, are the chickens in the chicken shack......

I see the situation like this.

> *The human race has been imprisoned as chickens in a chicken shack.*
> *The chickens are informed, through information passed down through the generations that they have only one life and they have to spend it in the chicken shack until the day they die. The alternative is that a clever chicken, a god chicken if you like, created their chicken shack in the first place and watches over them and judges them after they die. If they have been good in life they go on to live a better sort of chicken shack after they die. The opposite is true if they have been bad of course and if this is the case they will go to a worse chicken shack after they die. Their version of what we see as hell.*

The chickens don't know that crocodiles surround the chicken shack and are watching their every move.

The crocodiles themselves had actually created the story of the clever chicken that was suppose to have created the chicken shack and who would judge the inhabitants of the shack when they died. The Crocs also created the story of chickens having only one life.

The chickens spent so much of their time clucking at each other about dying after one life, or about the clever god like chicken judging them, that they never realised that the crocs even existed or that they had made the all story up. In fact neither version, death after one life nor the god like chicken was true. The crocs just wanted them not to discover who they really were, make them believe the lies, and to carry on producing eggs.

A couple of chickens ,who could see the crocs and what they did, tried to tell the rest of chickens that they had actually seen the crocs surrounding the chicken shack and that they knew chickens did not really die nor were they really going to be judged by a clever, god like, chicken after they died.

Sadly the chickens were too busy laying eggs and cleaning up their own chicken shit to listen!

Isn't it time we stopped clucking about and looked out of the symbolic window in chicken shack for once? If we cannot see through the window because of the filth that has been created by the chickens in the shack, then let us at least start looking at ways we can clean the window of the shack so we can see out of it. If the window is too high up the wall to reach inside the shack, then the chickens will have to join together to get *high* enough to see out of it. Maybe then we will have a clearer view of the crocodiles and have the ability to see exactly what they are doing?

Collective spiritual awareness will raise us as high as we want to go, far above the reach and the control of the Serpent Cult. So let's try to find the chicken shack window and clean it shall we? Maybe we are too scared, or too lazy, to look out of the chicken shack window because life in the chicken shack is not that bad really? Why spoil it?

Do we really have to sit there waiting for the rulers of the shack to bust in and hope that they strangle other chickens and eat them instead of busting in to strangle and eat us? That is exactly what we are doing at this present time on this planet, in this world. We sit there and watch the Serpent Cult create chaos in this world and butcher fellow human beings.

We just sit there like pathetic cowardly chickens in the shack watching the chicken next to us get slaughtered and yet we carry on laying eggs to feed the crocodiles. We have given our spiritual consent, given our power, to alien beings and we allow them to rule us.

Just how did / do we give our power away to the forces that covertly rule our planet?

We worship them that's how! I can see you nodding your head laughing, and thinking to yourself that you don't worship any aliens, and yes I agree you don't **knowingly** worship aliens but you worship them all the same. You are conned into doing so. Whether you are conned into it or not the result is the same, we give these aliens permission to rule us spiritually and physically. So they do just that.

Worshipping the Serpent is nothing new it has been going on for thousands of years. Things became clearer to me on this matter after I visited Dendera temple in Egypt, known as the Temple of Hathor. It is located north of Thebes (Luxor)

Anyway, as I have previously mentioned in "You Will Be Wiser When You're Older" and in other articles, I believe the human race is tricked into worshipping alien gods through very intelligent trickery and through their agencies, and agents living as humans on planet Earth. Alien agents on Earth, and the secret agencies they operate through, ensure that mankind is so deceptively tricked that the thought of being under the total spiritual control of aliens never enters the vast majority of human minds. Humans fail to comprehend the possibility that they may be being farmed.

I put this failure to comprehend or lack of ability to accept a situation on a par with someone being cheated on by their partner or by their husband or wife. The victim in this situation never seems to be aware that the love of their life is being unfaithful to them. This is especially so when the person cheating still proclaims love and respect for their partner, therefore deceiving their victim into believing they are still loyal.

The victim cannot see through the deception and wanders around totally oblivious to the fact that their partner is being unfaithful to them. Slight doubts that may appear in the victim's mind are cast aside, simply because it is more comfortable for them that way, a comfort zone that the victim does not want making uncomfortable. Even friends of the victim can hint that things are not as they seem but the victim refuses to take the hint. The victim still believes what he / she had heard from a usually trustable, loving and educating source.

Eventually the cheating partner will become exposed for what they are, a deceptive liar and the life of the victim is usually shattered because the illusion has been uncovered. The victim usually cannot believe how stupid he/ she could be for believing the lies in the first place. They feel so foolish. How could something they loved, trusted and believed so much turn out to be a pack of lies? They had convinced themselves that something they had been told was good and true when in reality what they had been told was bad and untrue. Those that have experienced deception from a loved one will know exactly what I am talking about. Ring any bells out there?

The same principle applies when trying to get people to believe the human race is being deceived on a massive scale by multidimensional beings and their agencies and their agents on Earth. We simply 'trust' our education and the system that has brought us up, just like we trust a loved one or a person in authority, especially teachers during childhood at school. We believe the experts and their versions of the meaning of life and the history of this world. It is easier for our comfort zone to do so and we don't like our comfort zone being entered by things we don't want to hear. Just like we wouldn't like to hear that our partner was being unfaithful to us.

> *"Errrr, excuse me but your wife/ husband is sleeping with another man / woman". "You have been lied to. I thought you should know the truth or at least investigate the matter"*
> *"Go away my wife/ husband wouldn't do that to me they told me they wouldn't and I believe them. So bugger off and take your lies with you"*

> *"Errrr, excuse me but you are being controlled by a Serpent Cult which controls all aspects of your life through their agents and agencies on Earth. You have been lied to. I thought you should know the truth or at least investigate the matter"*
> *"Go away, the church and my state education tells me this is not true and I believe them. So bugger off and take your lies with you. You are just a loony. "*

Comfort zone in the chicken shack? Yes?

It is easier for us to fob off comments we do not like to hear, things that will hurt us or things that sound just too ridiculous, but this does not mean they are not true.

....

Chapter 3
The Lotus Flower

"And if they stare
Just let them burn their eyes on you moving
And if they shout
Don't let it change a thing that you're doing
Hold your head up,
Hold your head up- high- woman
Hold your head up"

The lyrics are taken from the song 'Hold Your Head Up' by Argent

I need to mention the symbolism surrounding the lotus flower.

I don't want to drone on about Egyptian symbolism. I simply want to inform you of the symbolism connected to the official creation of this world, according to Serpent Cult's version of Egyptian history, and that can only be done by explaining the story of lotus flower and the ancient Egyptian version of creation.

If you are going to understand what I am saying in the later chapters of this book then it is essential that you read about the symbolism surrounding the lotus flower.

Sesen. A Lotus Flower.

This is a symbol of the Sun, of creation and rebirth. Because at night the flower closes and sinks underwater, at dawn it rises and opens again. According to one creation myth it was a giant lotus which first rose out of the watery chaos at the beginning of time. From this giant lotus the sun itself rose on the first day. A symbol of Upper Egypt .The lotus flower played a prominent role in the version of the creation story that originated in Heliopolis. Before the universe came into being, there was an infinite ocean of inert water which constituted the primeval being named Nun. Out of Nun emerged a lotus flower, together with a single mound of dry land. The lotus blossoms opened, and out stepped the self-created sun god, Atum, as a child.

A slightly different version of the creation story originated in Hermopolis. In that version, the sun god who formed himself

*from the chaos of Nun emerged from the lotus petals as Amen
Ra. The lotus is a flower which opens and closes each day. His
history went on to say that the petals of the lotus blossom
enfolded him when he returned to it each night.*
Source.www.kingtutshop.com/freeinfo/Lotus-Flower.htm

It is obvious to me and there is no doubt that the lotus flower (Sesen)
is very symbolic in Egypt. There is absolutely no doubt in my mind that
the lotus flower symbolises not only the birth of sun gods (Genesis let
there be light) but it also symbolises the Freemasonic motto 'order out of
chaos' (Ordo ab Chao).

There is also no doubt in my mind that high ranking Freemasons are
strongly linked to Serpent worship and indeed the brotherhood contains
alien agents amongst its own ranks. Serpent Cult agents operate and have
always operated through secret societies like the Freemasons, and of
course other old boy esoteric clubs, on Earth.

Jolly good chaps, they are definitely not, old bean.

Indeed the use of ancient Egyptian rituals inside secret societies is
rife.

So it is reasonable to say that the Masonic 'Order out of Chaos' motto is
based on lotus flower symbolism. Isn't it? 'From the chaos of the swamp
rose the lotus flower'.

What came out of the lotus flower?

I ask you to consider at this stage that *the chaos*, symbolised by the
muddy swamp, is a symbolic reference to planet Earth. Out of the lotus
flower came 'Ra' the sun god or light bringer. It is also symbolised that
the lotus flower also produced Atum (Amen), god of all creation. In
other words Ra and Atum were born as sun gods who were created *order*
out of chaos. They were literally created by, and living off the chaos.

The swamp (chaos) god is / was known as Nun. Nun ruled over the
chaos, after creating it. Nun was symbolically interpreted as being a
serpent. Nun must be the father or creator of Ra. In other words the sun
god was created and placed into this world by a Serpent.

Let us have a little look at NUN shall we?

The Egyptian god Nun
Illustration reproduced with kind permission from Ottar Vendel

*The snake god Nun was the personification of the swampy
water chaos (called Nun) from which the world emerged. From it
came four couples of serpents and frogs who represented - water,
infinite   time   darkness   and   void.*

*According to this myth from Hermopolis in Upper Egypt
finally formed during the last period of the Middle Kingdom,
Nun kept the solar boat of Ra floating by holding it up, and
onboard were the first gods (se also Hu and Sia). Sometimes
Kheper, the holy beetle, was in the middle holding the sun disk of
Ra, thereby symbolising resurrection and creation of the daylight
in the morning. Nun's wife was Nunet (also spelt Naunet, see
picture).*

*She was more obscure than her husband and could be seen
as a snake-headed woman who ruled the watery chaos.*
Source.www.kingtutshop.com/freeinfo/Lotus-Flower.htm

So, my little band of truth seekers, am I wrong to say that Nun was
the father or the creator of (Amen) Ra? The god who ruled the swamp,
the chaos, was indeed a serpent. The swamp spawned the sun gods
through the lotus flower.

It spawned order out of chaos.

The lotus flower symbolically behaved similar to the sun because it rose in the morning by coming out of the chaos (swamp) and returned to the swamp at night. This is similar to the sun rising and setting each day. Could this symbolise reptilians are not only controlling the *chaos* in this world but are also providing the agents (royal blood lines etc) to rule over us? Is it possible that the symbolism shown to you is indeed exactly that? Obviously Nun supports the solar boat, carrying the gods to dry land. Does this symbolise that reptilian gods support their agents?

I certainly believe so.

"Out of the lotus, created by the Eight, came forth Ra, who created all things, divine and human."

The Ogdoad

A group of gods from the Upper Egyptian town of Khemenu (Hermopolis) capital of nome 15 ("The Hare") in Middle Egypt. Thoth was the local main god who was considered to be the creator. The first gods he made (or made life possible for) were the eight reptiles of the Ogdoad (Greek for "group of eight") and they provided the elements which made life on earth possible.

They were:

Nun and Nunet :	**snakes, stood for water**
Heh and Hauhet :	**frogs, stood for infinite time**
Kek and Keket:	**snakes, stood for darkness**
Niau and Niaut:	**frogs, stood for void**

Snakes and Frogs: The Ogdoad.
Illustration reproduced with the kind permission of Ottar Vendel

The Egyptians believed that before the world was

formed, there was a watery mass of dark directionless chaos.
In this chaos lived the Ogdoad, four frog and four snake
deities of chaos. These deities were Nun and Naunet (water),
Amun and Amaunet (invisibility), Heh and Hauhet (infinity)
and Kek and Kauket (darkness).

It was from Nun that Ra joined with the sun god as Amen-Ra and
created himself, rising up on the first piece of land - the primeval mound
(Benben) out of the lotus blossom, born from the world egg, who then
found and landed on the mound. I will go into more detail about the
Benben later on. Please note that the Benben is the pyramid shape, used
amongst other things, as the top of Egyptian obelisks.

For now I want to mention a major event that took place in the
world in July 2005, the 'Live 8' music concerts. I wrote an article about
the Live 8 concerts shortly before the event took place, the article is
called "The Past is Calling" so I will be brief in my comments in this
book about it. I believe Live 8 was planned so that thousands of people
would be attracted to ancient sites such as the Circus Maximus in Rome,
the Brandenburg Gate area and Hyde Park etc. The people would then
be conned into taking part in a Serpent ritual.

Here is a picture of Live 8 organiser, Bob Geldof, and the Live 8
symbolic logo. The other picture is 'Ouroboros' the Serpent. Can you see
the similarity?

Bob Geldof and the Live 8 logo along with the Ouroboros

Is it possible that the 'eight', the snake goddesses and Nun etc,
mentioned in the quotation earlier, could somehow be 'symbolically'

connected to the Live 8 concerts that were held at very strategic locations around the world in July 2005.

I believe the Live 8 event was arranged by the Serpent Cult, using knighted stooges like Bob Geldof and they were covertly carrying out one of their numerous symbolic rituals. The Serpent Cult also conned the collective consciousness of mankind into joining in with it, through the mass media.

I just tell you the truth when I say the concerts were somehow symbolically announcing that the 8 are alive and are supporting the elite of this world just like they did thousands of years ago. The Live 8 celebrations, the singing, dancing and worship were somehow connected to ancient ritual and the whole Live 8 event was a covert scam. I don't pretend to know everything the ritual symbolised, I haven't all the answers, but I ask you to search inside yourself and ask yourself what was Live 8 all about?

The official version just does not add up to me. Was it really about poverty in Africa? Was it really arranged to create awareness about the poor and the starving? That is what we were told isn't it? Do you really think the term Live 8 was connected solely to the G8 Summit?

It is also an interesting fact that there were nine G8 summit leaders. Please try and find time to spend five minutes researching the *Heliopolitan Ennead* and you will find that there was also a group of nine gods known as the Heliopolitan Ennead in ancient Egypt. These gods swapped places with other gods to act as the nine ruling gods. The same thing applies to the G8 Summit leaders in my opinion. There were nine G8 summit leaders and they were symbolically supported by Live 8, exactly the same way as the Great 8 of creation supported the Ennead in ancient times. So when you add these facts together it doesn't sound so silly does it? The symbolism is there whether you think it is coincidence or not.

Here is a brief description of the Heliopolitan Ennead. It is also worth noting that the Eagle (Gleneagles) is also very symbolic to ancient Egypt and the USA.

The Ennead

The Ennead were the nine great Osirian gods Amen, Shu, Tefnut, Geb, Nut, Osiris, Isis, Set and Nephthys. The term is also used to describe the great council of the gods as well as a collective term for all the gods.

"The Great Nine", handled "all the important features of

Egyptian life; i.e., the sun, the atmosphere, the earth and sky, the underworld, etc. These gods form not only the nucleus of power, but also a court in which is judged the trials of gods."
Sourcewww.touregypt.net/godsofegypt/ennead.htm

Nothing much has changed then eh? Only these days the 'Great Nine' control all money, wars, drugs, poverty and mass murder. Nine corrupt agents running the world for the serpent?

The "nine" leaders at the G8 summit, posing for an official G8 photo. Are they the current modern day version of The Ennead?

I don't really think the Serpent Cult establishment gave a monkeys toss about poverty in Africa do you? They created it and they actually feed off the misery of the starving millions by doing so. Ask yourself now, 8 months after the event at the time writing this, if Africa is any better off or the human race is anymore aware about the real situation in Africa. In my opinion they are most definitely not.

The human race just went along with Live 8, blindly taking part in a ritual without even knowing or caring about it. The worship of rock or pop stars by the masses, the stars that are manipulated by the Serpent Cult anyway, will **never** stop oppression in Africa or anywhere else and by worshipping such idols the oppression will only increase.

The Serpent Cult use the pop industry to send out symbolic messages to the masses, usually these messages are sent subliminally, but most are blatant if you care to look, and it is just that the human race is too dumbed down to see what is actually going on.

I am saying that for some reason the Serpent Cult wanted thousands of people to celebrate Live 8 at certain ancient and some very symbolic locations around the globe, including the Diana memorial at London's Hyde Park.

The Diana memorial is located next to the Serpentine Lake in Hyde Park, London.

Live 8 took place leading up to and including the time when the nine leaders of the G8 summit sat on their arses at Gleneagles. Please also remember that the London Bombings (7/7) took place at the same time.

What amazes me most about Live 8 and I can't help laughing about it is that Bob Geldof was supposed to have arranged Live 8 armed only with a mobile phone and he was allegedly relying on the *goodwill* of various governments? All the concerts were free.

Now *come on*, could Bob really have arranged all this without any really long term planning and the total consent and assistance of the world's establishment? Geldof was supposed to have been seriously criticising the very countries, whose leaders were attending the G8 summit, for creating the poverty in Africa in the first place. So they just gave him free reign to party all over the world then? All for free?

The very people who helped create the poverty in Africa did it all out of the goodness of their hearts and appointed Bob Geldof as their figurehead, did they? Yes and I am a red assed Baboon!

In my opinion Bob Geldof is, in the least, a pawn in the Serpent Cult game of chess. The scenario we are expected to swallow is something like this isn't it?:..

Bob talking on his mobile phone to French and German governments...

> *"Hello there brothers, can I have your oldest and most historical venues, for free, to have a massive pop concert? Eiffel tower and the Brandenburg Gate will do for the initial announcement?*
>
> *The reply was obviously....Yes OK Bob but you may have to settle for Palais de Versailles and the Siegessäule. Both are very symbolic and are suitable for*

Serpent / Sun rituals. The first is the home of Louis the 14th who claimed to be the Sun god Apollo. The second is a park that used to be a royal hunting ground and is now known as Tiergarten ("animal garden"). It is the location of not only the Brandenburg Gate but the victory goddess on her victory column and it is placed on the Großer Stern (big star).

So yes please Bob, just send the thousands of people who are going to celebrate poverty by over eating, over drinking, and taking drugs to make themselves, and us, aware of the starving and dying people in Africa. We will clean up the mess after they all leave no problem and at no cost to you Bob"

(I wish I was joking!)

I have only given you brief details about the locations used at Live 8 please check them out for yourself. For starters try the Circus Maximus, Rome as one of the bigger sites or indeed a smaller event like the Eden Project in Cornwall. I am not saying people should not enjoy themselves whatever way they want to do. I enjoy taking part in a good knees-up myself. I just believe the good intentions of the masses, in relation to the live 8 pop concerts, were hijacked by the Serpent Cult and the masses have been duped into taking part in a massive Serpent Cult ritual disguised as charity pop concerts. Here is the poster used after the event for the cover of the DVD.

One Day One Concert One World

A New World order comes to my mind. Also just look at the mess left by the people attending the event in the other picture. This really does symbolically sum things up for me. People having stuffed their faces with junk food left this mess, whilst worshipping multi millionaire pop stars, and all this is supposed to have made us more aware of the starving in Africa?

The Aftermath: A pile of shit just like the official reasons for holding the event.

Yes making us aware of all the misery and death in Africa by stuffing our faces with Big Mac burgers and hotdogs while worshipping our idols.

Don't make me laugh. Or should I say don't make me cry?

I am sure the starving in Africa hoped the concerts were jolly nice and all those attending them had managed to get a glimpse of their favourite hero or heroine singing their latest song. Blind fools. Just what the fuck is going on out there?

I don't apologise for being passionate about this. Step back from the hype and look properly at the Live 8 events and think. For once in your life, just think. Just think.

I am saying as I indicated before the event actually took place, in my article '*The Past Is Calling*', that the concerts were created for worship, collective energy, focusing on certain symbolic areas around the globe. The fact that you can buy a DVD or CD of the event, to watch or listen, whilst the Africans still carry on dying, only adds insult to injury. Those people actually there and those watching on TV were taking part in what I believe was a sun god ritual. The vast majority of the world's population had some connection to the Live 8 concerts.

I was in Egypt in early July 2005 and Live 8 was even plastered all over the place there. You couldn't escape it. It was so vigorously promoted. I remember walking into a very grotty, very poor, bar in Luxor, there was literally horse shit all over the place but in contrast there was also a massive digital flat screen TV flashing away hung on a tree. It was booming out the concerts. I kid you not. The Live 8 concerts were repeatedly shown in Egypt.

The dates of the Live 8 concert and the G8 summit also need noting for reference to compare with information I will provide in a later chapter. The events lasted from the 2nd July to the 8th July. I will bring this matter up in a later chapter. Anyway I will get back on track.

I am also saying that the world we live in (our reality) has been hijacked by the Serpent just like the Live 8 concerts but on a much bigger scale. After hijacking our world the Serpent Cult put in place agents, rulers, for us to worship and obey. The symbolism tells us that Serpents prop up the solar boat of Amen Ra meaning, to me at least, that a Serpent Cult props up the world's elite. The same thing applies today as it did in ancient times in that multi-dimensional beings control the masses through their agents who pose as royalty and other VIP's.

Anyway, the Benben mentioned earlier is symbolic of a small mound of Earth sticking up out of the waters of chaos. It is the landing point where Nun, the Serpent, originally guided the solar boat and placed the sun god (elite) on dry land. That is why obelisks have the Benben stone (pointed pyramid shape) on top of the obelisk. It symbolises a piece of land sticking out of the water, the formation of dry stable land.

In common working class language this means the Benben stone is simply a marker point, a monumental announcement if you like, that the Serpent Cult own and rule the place where this marker point is actually located. It is on a par with sticking a stars and stripes flag in the moon. Does this information help you understand why obelisks are placed in strategic places, major cities, around the globe and that is why these obelisks *carry* the Benben stone? It should do.

London, Paris, Washington and even the Pope's luxurious penthouse, the Vatican, has a bloody great big obelisk stuck outside it, complete with a Benben stone. Is the penny starting to drop?

All the obelisks were taken from the ancient lands and placed in all areas of the world. They are symbolic marker points linked to the ancient sun god temples. They are literally important parts of a sun god temple and by placing the obelisks around the world it symbolises that the ancient sun temple has officially been spread all over the world.

Does Big Ben's clock tower, a giant stone obelisk with a Benben shaped top, which is located in London, make more sense to you now? It marks the centre, the HQ if you like, of the Serpent Cult.

Big Ben, or should I call it Big Benben, also symbolises the *centre of time* for the Serpent Cult. That is why the rest of the world set their clocks to GMT.

The masses were fed bullshit about why the clock tower is called Big Ben claiming it was simply the name of the bell. I know it sounds initially ludicrous for you to hear that Big Ben is a giant symbolic Benben stone, but that is exactly what it is.

Big Ben is globally accepted as being the centre of time in this world. Hence the silly farce of changing our clocks every six months.

When you turn your clocks back or forward you connect your subconscious to the Serpent Cult's Benben stone (Big Ben). This keeps the illusion of time firmly fixed in the collective consciousness of mankind. We consciously and subconsciously submit to the powers of the Benben stone that represents the sun gods. In other words it is just one big hypnotists watch!!! What the masses think they get- they get

Big Ben: A giant symbolic Benben

You must turn this back and forward when told to. They need to keep you hypnotised you see! Can you grasp what I am saying? I am not the first to mention the illusion of time, other researchers have mentioned this.

I realise that the majority of us didn't have a clue what a Benben stone was. Nobody taught me anything about the Benben stone at school nor did they tell me that the Pope, who is portrayed as God's number one, God's right hand man, God's personal assistant, God's best buddy and some kind of angelic goody two-shoes all rolled into one, has a giant obelisk of his own outside his penthouse in Vatican City either. Did they tell you this at school? Did they bloody hell as like!

Anyway, I also always used to wonder why the ancient Pharaohs wore the *Uraeus*, a crown, which was decorated with the head of raised cobra. I have come to realise that it symbolises 'Serpent control of the mind' and of course also symbolises the Serpent Cult's protection of its own agents on Earth. In other words it protects its royal and presidential puppets of this world such as Elizabeth the second and George W Bush who are both controlled and protected by the Serpent Cult. They are a family of vipers that slithered out of the same nest. The snazzy head band, illustrated below, symbolises this. The crowns and other royal jewels, worn by modern day royals, are just updated versions of the same symbolism. Things like the Koh-I-Noor diamond, which simply means 'Mountain of Light', are also used for symbolic purposes and used in ritual but, sadly, the masses are just too dumbed down to notice.

The Royal Uraeus

The Royal Ureaus Crown
Picture reproduced with kind permission from Ottar Vendel

This figure (above) is seen wearing the Royal Ureaus Crown, also referred to as the sacred serpent crown. Maybe this is better explained by mentioning some symbolic headwear worn by the masses. I wear a football bobble hat and a football scarf. These items openly show the symbolism of my favourite football team. I announce my mentality and show the entire world where my spiritual loyalty belongs when I wear them.

The same can be said for fire helmets worn by firemen or police helmets worn by policemen. The same scenario applies to military personnel etc.
For example a captain of a ship wears a captains sailing hat, a pilot wears a flight captain's hat and so on. All hats will openly and symbolically declare the mentality or the intentions of the person wearing them. They also obviously wear the emblem of whomever they obey. Well don't they?
The policeman always wears the emblem of the force he obeys, same situation also applies for fireman and pilots etc. They display their authority and power. The raised serpent symbolism on the Pharaoh's sacred serpent crown is just the same. There is no difference whatsoever.

Serpent headwear is also worn by the Pope indeed it is another blatant example. The picture below shows the Pope and what I believe to be Serpent symbolism or at least *head* of the Serpent symbolism. The Templar cross is also used in this case. This cross has nothing to do with Jesus. It's all a deception and another con trick performed by the multidimensional beings that covertly rule us. The Pope's hat is blatant sun god and serpent symbolism in my opinion. You won't get the local priest telling you these things though.

The Pope wears his hat and scarf for the exact same reasons that the football fan wears the same. They are simply declaring their connection and allegiance to the thing they believe in. They willingly flaunt the relevant emblem because they worship whatever the emblems represent. They bare their colours so to speak. The same rule applies for the King or the Queen or the puppet presidents and politicians. Obviously these days any serpent worship rituals, those most blatant anyway, are most likely carried out down   a Masonic lodge or at secret outdoor locations like Bohemian Grove. That is not to say that the public is not subjected to other Serpent rituals taking place right under their noses and of course, the Catholic and Protestant churches carry them out all the time.

The Pope bearing his colours: Serpent robes.

Please follow with your eyes, the Popes scarf upwards towards the hat. Now then! Is that the shape of a Serpent? Well isn't it? Go on look again more closely. If you cannot see a serpent, snake or some other sort of 'slippery customer' then please ring Lancashire Health Care NHS trust in Preston, Lancashire, UK and tell them Matthew Delooze is hallucinating and seeing serpent symbolism hidden in the Pope's, Sunday best, hat and scarf or whatever he calls it. I call it his snake suit. The hat is obviously a Serpents head and it symbolises Serpent control of the mind through religion in my opinion.

Is it a bird? Is it a plane?..No it is Serpentman…The King of child sex abuse and Luciferic ritual.

Snakes alive: The Pope in his snake suit.

The point I am trying to make in this chapter, and future ones, is that same rules apply today as they did in Ancient Egypt. The masses are enslaved by the ruling elite and that ruling elite are also masters of deception. The world's elite are masked snakes in royal and religious clothing, if you like, and they are deceiving the masses into enslaving themselves. Agents for multi-dimensional alien beings are deceiving the masses into some sort of spiritual surrender.

It is time to set yourself free.

....

Chapter 4:
The Weeping Queen.

"Did you ever see a woman
coming out of New York City
with a frog in her hand?
I did, don't you know,
I did don't you know
and don't it show."

The lyrics are taken from the song 'New York City' by T. Rex

I would like to stay with the Benben stone (pyramid capstone), and Big Ben in London just for a little longer. I would like to point out some symbolism and explain how the masses are duped into carrying out rituals. Let us start with the words, written in Latin, actually engraved on Big Ben:

'DOMINE SALVAM FAC REGINAM NOSTRAM VICTORIAM PRIMAM'

Officially this means "Lord save our Queen Victoria first." or "God save our Queen Victoria the First." Obviously the manipulation of ambiguous languages and phrases could be and is regularly abused by the Serpent Cult.

Most of us have an education that is absolutely worthless to us. Indeed we are only rewarded for our education if we actually go along with the system that created it. If you agree with the education that has been forced on you then you will be allowed to carve out a profession via that same education but this is only because you will strengthen a corrupt system.

Most professionals know their profession is a sham but they go along with the bullshit for the material security it brings. Sooner or later though the *education* they blindly follow will make them hit a spiritual brick wall. There is no escaping the self judgment we will all have to face one day, no matter how many credit cards you have. I don't mean we will meet a bully boy bouncer at the illusionary pearly gates when we die, I mean we will self assess ourselves one day.

What will your excuse be then eh?

I received my education from Burnley Borough Council, that's why I am such a bad writer, until I was placed in the care of the local authorities aged thirteen. They sent me to a care home and reform school. I learnt more by reading the back of a Cornflakes box between the ages of five and thirteen, than I did whilst I was literally being brainwashed in the state school education system. To the brainwashed eye, the average member of the public, this means the authorities were meant to care for me from the age of thirteen to eighteen. The public may assume that when a child is placed in care that they will be properly cared for. In reality I was placed under the total control of some of the most corrupt organisations in the country, namely Burnley Borough Council and Lancashire County Council.

The Serpent Cult controls all local councils, and the faceless liars and fraudsters they employ, to keep the lid on things behind the scenes.

The vast majority of sexual, mental and physical abuse is carried out on children by officials working in care homes and through official local authority organizations and their employees, including the church and church officials. Children from care homes and approved schools were/are supplied as sex toys and punch bags to high rankers in authority, to use and abuse at their will. A few stories were made pubic by the victims of abuse recently, dating back to the 70's and 80's, but it is only the tip of the iceberg. The kids I saw in care were the most vulnerable people in this world and usually, surprisingly to some, despite their dire situation they would have given you the shirt of their back if you needed it.

Anyway back to Big Ben.

Despite me being as thick as two short planks I offer you my own translation of the words etched on the obelisk that you know as Big Ben and in my opinion they are roughly:

"Master save with ease the Queen of Our Victory as soon as possible"

('DOMINE SALVAM FAC REGINAM NOSTRAM VICTORIAM PRIMAM')

Obviously the Benben stone caps this clock tower (obelisk.) I don't believe that the words written on Big Ben had anything to do with Queen Victoria as you know her. It is simply another deception and a play on ambiguous words. It is a covert symbolic announcement; mind you it's not really covert is it? Its just we are too blind, or too lazy to see it.

I believe the words on Big Ben refer symbolically to Isis the Egyptian Queen and not Victoria. The Serpent Cult erect many 'victory goddess' monuments similar to the one in Berlin and used in the Live 8 concert ritual mentioned in the last chapter. I believe the wording in Latin on Big Ben to honour a Sun Goddess.

The Victory Goddess monument in Berlin that is connected to Live 8.

The term *As soon as possible* in my version of the motto on Big Ben refers to the time and has nothing to do with Victoria being named Victoria the 1st and "time" is totally controlled by the Serpent Cult anyway. The entire world follows GMT and Big Ben is the symbolic face for GMT. Victoria was never known as "Victoria the First" anyway. In my opinion the inscription on Big Ben is symbolically praising Isis as a victorious queen and is a monument to her as a victory goddess. The reference to as soon as possible is in my opinion linked to the creation of a New World Order and that is the aim of the Serpent Cult which they want *'as soon as possible'*. I believe the masses automatically run away from Latin language and literature. We have been mentally and spiritually programmed to do so.

Isn't Latin so silly? It is so boring and useless isn't it? So let's not touch it with a barge pole eh? The collective thought that is embedded in our subconscious is to stay clear from Latin isn't it? So we bloody well do just that don't we?

The establishment could write in Latin "you are all a set of stupid bastards" on monuments or coins for that matter and we wouldn't have a clue. Well would we? Those few that think they know Latin should remember they can only repeat what they were taught. I have no doubt my translation of the words on Big Ben would be scoffed at by Latin experts. I don't give a monkey's.

Widespread ignorance of translation and understanding Latin, amongst the masses is part of the Serpent Cult agenda to enslave mankind. Latin is used as a deceptive code to covertly announce things, especially on coins.

Other things can also be used to symbolically announce things to the ignorant masses, especially when the royal bloodlines are used for reference and to endorse the events.

Queen Victoria and her husband Albert worked hard for the Serpent Cult and they carried out many symbolic events during their time. They also had nine children. These children spread the royal bloodline, therefore spread Serpent Cult representatives, throughout the world. Victoria was known as the 'Weeping Queen' or 'The Queen that mourned for 40 years' after the death of Albert in 1861. Indeed she is known throughout the world as a famous weeping widow dressed in black. I am not amused to say, the black widow wept and lived in the wilderness for 40 years. Her husband, Albert, was not allowed to be an official Freemason, not in public anyway. That said Victoria insisted that her sons, including Edward, were Freemasons. All the members of Royal Family are connected to secret societies. Indeed Victoria herself played mum to young girls and she was made Chief Patroness of the Masonic Girls School in 1882!

Prince Albert was allegedly responsible for introducing the Christmas tree into this country. I have written one or two articles about Christmas already. They are available for viewing at the website listed at the end of this book.

I would like to spend a couple of paragraphs mentioning the Christmas tree. Firstly the paragraph below is from the 'London News' regarding the first Christmas tree to appear in Windsor Castle 1841. The Christmas tree was introduced by Prince Albert.

> *"The tree employed for this festive purpose," says the*
> *News, "is a young fir about eight feet high, and has six*
> *tiers of branches. On each tier, or branch, are arranged*

*a dozen wax tapers. Pendent from the branches are
elegant trays, baskets, bonbonnieres, and other
receptacles for sweetmeats, of the most varied and
expensive kind; and of all forms, colours, and degrees of
beauty. Fancy cakes, gilt gingerbread and eggs filled with
sweetmeats, are also suspended by variously coloured
ribbons from the branches. The tree, which stands upon
a table covered with white damask, is supported at the
root by piles of sweets of a larger kind, and by toys and
dolls of all descriptions, suited to the youthful fancy, and
to the several ages of the interesting scions of Royalty for
whose gratification they are displayed. The name of each
recipient is affixed to the doll, bonbon, or other present
intended for it, so that no, difference of opinion in the
choice of dainties may arise to disturb the equanimity of
the illustrious juveniles. On the summit of the tree
stands the small figure of an angel, with outstretched
wings, holding in each hand a wreath.".....*

This is another paragraph from the same article......,

*Once a Christmas tree had been set up in Windsor
Castle, you may be sure that Christmas trees blazed
and twinkled in every British household that could
afford one. It has remained ever since just what it is with
us, the centre of all the Christmas festivities.*

**Queen Victoria's Christmas tree at Windsor in 1850 as painted by James Roberts
(1824 - 1867). The presents around the tree are from Prince Albert.**
The Royal Collection © 2003, Her Majesty Queen Elizabeth II

Prince Albert is obviously credited with bringing the Christmas tree inside the homes of the British people. Apparently the tradition, or the spark that set this fashion off, stems from Germany. The modern day Christmas tree was also introduced to the USA by German immigrants. Dutch settlers landing at New York (New Amsterdam) had previously introduced Santa Klaus. Santa Claus is the Dutch diminutive (or pet name) for Saint Nicholas, and Saint Nicholas is the patron saint of boys and girls. The foundations for the modern day Christmas celebrations had been laid in the western world by the late 19th century. These foundations led to Christmas being celebrated as it is today.

I will just point out one or two popular interpretation of the history of the Christmas tree, and then I will give you my opinion. The St. Boniface Story is one version, it is a story about a monk who went to Germany from the UK to teach the word of God. Legend has it that he used the triangular shape of the fir tree to symbolise the Holy Trinity of God the Father, Son and Holy Spirit. It is said St Boniface converted people to accept the fir tree as God's tree instead of the oak tree. Previously the oak free was symbolic of the tree of life or God's tree of life. The reason St Boniface did this was because came upon a group of pagans who had gathered around an oak tree and were preparing to sacrifice a child to the gods of farming or agriculture. St Boniface was said to have destroyed the oak tree and stopped the sacrifice and saved the child. A small fir tree sprang up in its place, which Saint Boniface told the pagans was the 'Tree of Life' and represented the life of Christ. From there it appears the use of a Christmas tree indoors spread from Germany. German Christians would bring trees into their homes to decorate. In some areas evergreen trees were scarce so the families would build a 'Christmas pyramid' which was a simple wooden structure which they decorated with branches and candles.

The tradition of the Christmas tree eventually spread throughout Europe. The Royal family help popularise the tree in England by decorating the first Christmas tree at Windsor Castle in 1841. Prince Albert decorated the first English Christmas Tree with candles, candies, fruits, and gingerbread.

Where exactly did the Germans get their ideas about Christmas trees from?

It is also said that the Druids of ancient England and France allegedly decorated oak trees with fruit and candles (symbolically baring gifts and worshipping it) to honour their gods of harvests. It is said that human sacrifices were also made under the oak tree.

Where did the druids get their ideas from? Consider this?

The Romans also decorated trees with trinkets and candles at a festival known as Saturnalia. These celebrations were around winter solstice time and were carried out to honour Saturn, the roman god of agriculture. Saturnalia is basically an older version of our modern day Christmas and trees were also used in this ritual.

Apparently Saturnalia became one of the most popular Roman festivals in ancient Rome and during the festival masters and slaves switch places which led to widespread drinking and debauchery. The customary greeting for the occasion is to chant "Io, Saturnalia!" — *io* (pronounced "yo") being a Latin interjection related to "ho" as in "Ho, praise to Saturn"

Another festival linked to Saturnalia was the festival for *Sol Invictus*. Here is a brief description of the festival for Sol Invictus from the wikipedia website.

> **Sol Invictus** ("the unconquered sun") or, more fully, **Deus Sol Invictus** ("the unconquered sun god") was a religious title applied to three distinct divinities during the later Roman Empire
>
> Unlike the earlier, agrarian cult of Sol Indiges (the sun in-the-earth"), the title *Deus Sol Invictus* was formed by analogy with the imperial titulature *pius felix invictus* ("dutiful, fortunate, unconquered").
>
> A festival of the birth of the unconquered sun (or *Dies Natalis Solis Invicti*) was celebrated when the duration of daylight first begins to increase after the winter solstice- the rebirth of the sun.

Deus Sol Invictus ("the undefeated sun god")

It is obvious to me that the use of the Christmas tree is symbolically linked to the biblical *tree of life*. I have said in previous articles that I believe the Christmas tree is symbolic of the Serpent in the tree in the Garden of Eden. I believe Christmas tree is linked to literally worshipping the serpent, through carrying out rituals linked to sun gods.

I also believe the *angel* that we place on top of our Christmas trees symbolises the image of the sun goddess Isis and other sun deities. Indeed inscribed in the temple of Isis on the island of Philae in Egypt;

> *"I, Isis, am all that has been, that is or shall be; No mortal man hath ever me unveiled. The fruit which I have brought forth is the 'SUN'."*

Is it possible that we are deceived into carrying out an act of sun god worship every Christmas? Are we unknowingly carrying out ancient rituals in the guise of celebrating Christmas? I certainly say we are, indeed I am convinced of it. I am totally convinced that we unknowingly worship the Serpent by placing trees in our homes.

We also symbolically leave gifts under the tree, just like they did in ancient sun god rituals that have nothing to do with Christianity. This act has replaced, but is still symbolic, of the sacrificial gifts that the ancients left under the tree in the past to appease their god's. Nothing has changed really but we cannot seem to see what's going on under our noses.

Food or tasty tit bits were placed on "Ritual Trees" simply to symbolise the eating fruits from the biblical tree of life or the forbidden fruits from the tree of knowledge, after being tempted by the Serpent.

The fruits of the tree are symbolised these days with little shaped chocolates wrapped in silver or gold paper. I also believe that *tinsel* used on Christmas trees is also direct Serpent symbolism. Tinsel was invented in Germany around 1610. Real silver was used and machines were invented which produced the wafer thin strips of silver especially to be used as tinsel. Obviously when you put a long thin strip of tinsel on the tree it looks like a snake.

Is it so strange to believe that somehow a plot was hatched to get the masses to carry out Serpent or a sun god ritual by getting them to place symbolic trees in their homes? Obviously if this is true then the masses somehow had to be conned into placing these symbolic trees in their homes in the first place. Tales like the St Boniface story could be partly true or total bullshit. Queen Victoria and Albert may have innocently set the symbolic fashion for Christmas trees in the UK. It does not really matter. The vast majority of the masses in the western world now have symbolic trees in their homes every winter solstice and the vast majority of us haven't a clue why. Obviously the masses were covertly led from using the symbolic oak tree into using the symbolic fir tree or we would all have great lumbering oak trees in our homes every Christmas!

Using the fir tree to replace the oak tree didn't affect the symbolism. Indeed the pyramid-shaped Christmas tree is now the official symbol that has been placed in the collective consciousness of mankind and it is now the fir tree that officially represents the tree of life. It has completely replaced the oak tree in physical form but the symbolism stays the same. We are literally still carrying out the festival of Sol Invictus from ancient times. It's just that we have been conned into thinking we are carrying out a Christian ritual instead. We are carrying out sun god ritual but it is hidden behind silly fairy tales about baby Jesus. We are unknowingly celebrating the rebirth of a sun god (our enslaver) and not the birth of any saviour. False history books and ambiguous scriptures along with the use of very deceptive trickery have helped this happen. Its time you woke up to the deception.

Going back to the Saturnalia festival again, it is said that everyone used the term "Io Saturnalia" (Io pronounced Yo) and the term is linked to the Latin word Ho as in "Ho praise to Saturn".

Does this ring a bell with any of you when I remind you that the words or the term "ho ho ho" or "yo ho ho" are used a lot during the Christmas period, especially when linked to Santa Clause while he rings his bell? Does this not indicate that you could be really symbolically praising Saturn, the sun god, and not some saviour known as the Christ, during the Christmas period?

The question regarding the use of 'Latin' arises again doesn't it? Are the masses being exploited because of their ignorance in understanding Latin and, of course, other symbolism connected to it? I strongly believe this is true.

Saturnalia was also a time for heavy drinking and a lot of sexual activity took place. That is why the typical office Christmas party or the average works Christmas party encourages its staff to behave like idiots at them. It is all part of the ritual and the excuse to get drunk and have sex at Christmas time is embedded in the collective consciousness of the human race.

There is absolutely no difference between the ancient Romans having orgies during Saturnalia or modern day people having sex at Christmas parties. Well is there? The human race, especially in the western world has been conditioned to drink and have sex at Christmas time yet they cannot see that they have been hypnotised to carry out such things. It is all about releasing spiritual energy at the time of the rebirth of the Sun. There is no other reason for it whatsoever. Wake up. Think hard and wake up.

. . . .

Chapter 5
Made it Ma...Top of the Flag Pole

"Made it Ma...Top of the world!"

Quote from the movie 'White Heat' starring James Cagney.

I'd like to leave the dusty road to Dendera for a moment but I will return to it in the next chapter. I would like to mention an experience I had in my late teens. Nay I can be more accurate than that. It was shortly after the Queens Silver Jubilee celebrations took place in June 1977. I was 18 years and three months old in June 1977 when the streets celebrated the Queens Silver Jubilee.

I experienced what I can only describe as an out-of-body experience in June 1977 and I would like to tell you about it but first I will explain what was going on at the time regarding the Queens silver jubilee. I quote from the official royal website below...

The actual anniversary of The Queen's accession was on 6 February but the full jubilee celebrations began in the summer of 1977.

On 4 May at the Palace of Westminster both Houses of Parliament presented loyal addresses to The Queen, who in her reply stressed that the keynote of the jubilee was to be the unity of the nation.

During the summer months The Queen did a large scale tour, having decided that she wished to mark her jubilee by meeting as many "of her people" as possible. No other Sovereign had visited so much of Britain in the course of just three months - the six jubilee tours in the UK and Northern Ireland covered 36 counties. The home tours began in Glasgow on 17 May 1977. The tours continued throughout England and Wales before culminating in a visit to Northern Ireland.

Official overseas visits were also made to Western Samoa, Australia, New Zealand, Tonga, Fiji, Tasmania, Papua New Guinea, Canada and the West

Indies. During the year it was estimated that The Queen and The Duke of Edinburgh travelled 56,000 miles.

The climax of the national celebrations came in early June. On the evening of Monday 6 June, The Queen lit a bonfire beacon at Windsor which started a chain of beacons across the country. On Tuesday 7 June, vast crowds saw The Queen drive in the Gold State Coach to St Paul's Cathedral for a Service of Thanksgiving attended by heads of state from around the world and former prime ministers of the UK

Afterwards The Queen and members of the Royal Family attended a lunch at the Guildhall, in which The Queen made a speech. She declared, "My Lord Mayor, when I was twenty-one I pledged my life to the service of our people and I asked for God's help to make good that vow. Although that vow was made in my salad days, when I was green in judgement, I do not regret nor retract one word of it."

An estimated 500 million people watched on television as the procession returned down the Mall. Back at Buckingham Palace The Queen made several balcony appearances. Street parties and village parties started up all over the country: in London alone 4000 were reported to have been held.

The final event of the central week of celebrations was a river progress down the Thames from Greenwich to Lambeth on Thursday 9 June, emulating the ceremonial barge trips of Elizabeth I. After The Queen had opened the Silver Jubilee Walkway and the new South Bank Jubilee Gardens, the journey ended with a firework display, and a procession of lighted carriages took The Queen back to Buckingham Palace for more balcony appearances to a cheering crowd.....

So you can understand that the official version of events indicates that millions of union jack flags and literally miles of jubilee bunting was being used both here in the UK and the rest of the commonwealth. Other symbolism involving the establishment and the Serpent Cult is also there for all to see. If you want to look that is.

Firstly let's start with historical meaning of the 'Jubilee'. It may enlighten you as to the true reasons why millions of people were conned into waving flags and having street parties whilst celebrating the Jubilee.

The Royal Jubilee ritual dates back to ancient Egypt. Nothing new there then! It was known as the Heb-Sed festival and it was usually celebrated around thirty years into a king's rule and thereafter, every three years. The Heb-Sed festival (ritual) symbolized regeneration and was meant to assure a long reign in the Pharaoh's afterlife. The Heb-Sed ritual was meant to bring back the harmony between the king and the universe, in the case of illness or just old age of the king the ritual was simply carried out to bring rejuvenation. The official rituals were supposed to be performed after thirty years of a king's reign, but there is evidence that the festival was sometimes scheduled earlier.

So based on the Heb-Sed ritual, which the silver jubilee was based on, the Queen was obviously carrying out a ritual *for her own benefit* and not a ritual to *unite the nation* and to *meet as many subjects as she could*, as it is claimed in the official version of events. Indeed the Heb-Sed celebration in ancient Egypt was a performance, a 'run and dance' ritual, aimed at proving that the King or Queen was still physically able to rule the country, an ancient fitness test so to speak. In carrying out this test the King was also suppose to be "rejuvenated and reborn." Just like the Sun.

Now then, just consider for a moment the fact that the Queen and Prince Philip did carry out some kind of a fitness test ritual when celebrating the silver jubilee. Indeed the history surrounding the Heb-Sed indicates that they most certainly did. Here is another quote from official royal website...

> No other Sovereign had visited so much of Britain in the course of just three months - the six jubilee tours in the UK and Northern Ireland covered 36 counties. The home tours began in Glasgow on 17 May 1977.
>
> The tours continued throughout England and
>
> Wales before culminating in a visit to Northern Ireland.
>
> Official overseas visits were also made to Western Samoa, Australia, New Zealand, Tonga, Fiji, Tasmania, Papua New Guinea, Canada and the West Indies. During the year it was estimated that The Queen and the Duke of Edinburgh travelled 56,000 miles.....

Well I'll go to Timbuktu, scratch my arse, and come back again. Does this information not indicate, even to the most sceptical of us, that the Queen was proving astronomical *fitness* to rule?

Too bloody right it does, well done Ma'am.

I do not blush when I say 56,000 miles travelled by an agent for the Serpent Cult in a Heb-Sed or Jubilee ritual ensures she will be *reborn* to rule over us again. Please check out the Heb-Sed ritual and its links to modern day royalty on the internet and ask yourself why Elizabeth carried out an ancient Egyptian ritual in the UK? Is it possible that the ritual has been passed down through the Serpent Cult blood line? This ritual has obviously spread from the ancient Sumerian and Babylonian lands but why does it carry on today? Just who the hell is arranging and organising such things?

Why are modern day silver jubilees connected to ancient Egypt rituals, such as Heb-Sed, anyway? The answer in my opinion is simple, as I have mentioned in previous articles, it is a case of 'what the masses think they get- they get'.

The Heb-Sed, silver jubilee, ritual was carried out to increase collective spiritual acceptance of the Queen as your ruler. The Queen is an agent for a Serpent race of multi-dimensional beings that covertly rule this planet. Therefore the increase in collective *spiritual* acceptance from the masses, created by such rituals is to achieve official *physical* acceptance from the masses, of the Serpent Cult as a whole as well as the Queen individually. Simply put, the vast majority of minds have accepted the Queen and her masters as an official ruling body in this world.

Those waving 'flags' at such celebrations were literally adding bars to the spiritual prison we live in. The same things happen around the planet with other members of Royal families and Presidents etc. The same Serpent Cult clique are carrying out the same rituals all over the planet repeatedly but the masses haven't a clue what is really going on and blindly join in.

It is estimated that over 500 million people witnessed the silver jubilee celebrations just on TV alone. These people accepted the Queen as their ruler or as a foreign ruler whether they agreed with it or not. Again what we are made to think becomes our reality. What the masses think they get-they get. We think Elizabeth is our Queen so Elizabeth is our ruler and we give our mind and spiritual energy to her as a result.

The Queen carried out another ritual during the Jubilee celebrations Does anyone know the real reason why the Queen had to light a bonfire beacon on the evening of the 6th June 1977 at Windsor and why it led to a chain of official beacons being lit across the UK? The day after, on

June 7th 1977, she travelled in her gold coach to meet the official heads of state and all previous British prime ministers that are still alive. There is obviously more to this burning of fires than meets the eye and I also believe the gold coach that was used by the Queen, and previous Serpent Cult agents, symbolises the vessels used in ancient Egyptian ritual including the 'solar boat'. Here is a picture of the Queens coach.

The Queen's gold coach. Could it be a symbolic ancient solar boat?

Take a look at the illustration (below) from ancient Egypt showing another festival ritual known as the festival of Opet. The ancient kings and queens of Egypt used to carry out their ritual in symbolic solar boats to symbolise travelling with Ra in the solar boat held by Nun, as mentioned in chapter three. Here is an image of a solar boat taken from a papyrus I bought in Egypt.

Is the Queens gold coach just an updated version of the ancient Egyptian solar boat?

In my opinion there is absolutely no difference between the transport used by an ancient sun god worshipping Pharaoh and the transport used by a modern day sun loving Queen. They were both agents operating within the Serpent Cult to deceive the human race. Ask yourself why modern day royalty behave just like the ancient kings of Egypt did?

Anyway going back to the silver jubilee or Heb-Sed, twenty five years on the throne being treated like a goddess is obviously no mean feat and does indeed deserve recognition, if only for fooling the masses for so long. Surely a bunch of flowers and a few cards is enough isn't it? That's all we get at the most isn't it? So why does the Queen have to travel around the bloody planet doing strange things everywhere? In my opinion the population played victim to a large dose of mass hypnosis in 1977. Even those who are consciously against the royal family could not escape being duped into joining in the ritual in some way.

Most people joined in with the ritual even if it was only by taking an extra day's holiday from work. This would make you at least think that the Queen was being nice. You could have innocently joined in the ritual just by buying a pack of biscuits and eating them because a special edition wrapper depicting the Queen was especially printed for the Jubilee. Everything from mars bars to an egg cup had the silver jubilee message on it and this was no coincidence because the masses had in someway to join in the ritual for the ritual to be *spiritually* valid.

**Everyone joined in with the silver jubilee (Heb-Sed) in some way.
A jubilee *mug*-just like you and me!**

I realise you may think these things are unimportant but I assure you they are not. They are definitely important. All the things mentioned affect your own individual subconscious and even the act of nibbling your way through jubilee biscuits, drinking tea from a jubilee mug or just going down the pub on the special holiday you got indicate that you joined in and endorsed the ritual. The effect on collective consciousness is enormous when these things happen. In 1977 the emphasis was placed on creating street parties and the masses blindly arranged thousands of them all over the country and the commonwealth.

It may be easier for younger people to understand what I am saying if I mention the death of Princess Diana as a more modern and better example of how royal events affect the collective consciousness of mankind.

Mass celebrations or mass mourning has a very big effect on the mass consciousness of the human race because our emotions create mass spiritual energy, especially when we all feel the same way at the same time. Certain events can be exploited to the fullest by the Serpent Cult to create spiritual energy. They can create mass emotional celebrations for rebirth rituals (such as the Jubilee) or mass emotional mourning for sacrificial rituals (such as the ritual murder of Princess Diana). The Serpent Cult can create any situation it wants to suit the type of spiritual energy it requires. So if The Serpent Cult was to receive respect energy to endorse the power of an agent, in this case the Queen, it will arrange for something like a Heb-Sed ritual to take place and get the masses to emotionally support it. Therefore when the masses accept and endorse the rule of the agent (the Queen) over them they also accept and endorse the power of the force that controls the agent. The force that controls the Queen as their puppet is a force of multi-dimensional alien beings.

The Serpent Cult *controls* how the majority of people in the human race will feel emotionally at certain times. They literally feed off our emotions so it is very much in their interest to control how we feel. They simply get us to symbolically worship and emotionally respect VIP's because these actions actually create energy.

Even those that are totally against the royal family are deceived into worshipping them. One way of conning the masses is by the use of subliminal messages. This can be done in many ways. The most obvious way is through cash, paper notes and coins that bear the faces of Serpent Cult agents. Yes even that silly note or coin from some foreign land is a hypnotic con trick to somebody, somewhere. Postage stamps, pop music, school hymns and movies are all used to get you to accept and agree to Serpent Cult control. Can you understand that every time you spend money you are showing emotional connection to the faces printed on the notes? The respect for money creates spiritual energy and the energy that is created goes to feed the images on the money.

I must mention a conversation that I had the other day with an ageing punk rocker from the seventies. He told me he had been anti-royalty for decades. He also told me about the Sex Pistols song God Save The Queen that came out in 1977 to try and hi-jack the jubilee celebrations and create, what punk rockers were suppose to create, anarchy.

Everyone was led to believe how free they were. How couldn't they be free if songs like 'God Save the Queen' by the Sex Pistols are allowed to be produced? Indeed I believe the song was barred from most radio stations at least for a while during the jubilee celebrations. This obviously led to a situation in which more people (anti-royals) started to buy the song. Because of the increase in sales the record reached number two in the charts, obviously more people bought it and listened to it because of the ban and the attention it received because of the ban. This was no coincidence either.

Here are the lyrics to the Sex Pistols "God Save the Queen"

God save the Queen
the fascist regime,
they made you a moron
a potential H-bomb.

God save the Queen
she ain't no human
being.
There is no future
in England's dreaming

Don't be told what you
want
Don't be told what you
need.
There's no future
there's no future
there's no future for you

God save the Queen
we mean it man
we love our queen
God saves

God save the Queen
'cos tourists are money
and our figurehead
is not what she seems

Oh God save history
God save your mad
parade
Oh Lord God have
mercy
all crimes are paid.

When there's no future
how can there be sin
we're the flowers
in the dustbin
we're the poison
in your human machine
we're the future
you're future

God save the Queen
we mean it man
we love our queen
God saves

God save the Queen
we mean it man
there is no future
in England's dreaming

OK. On the face of it appears that the lyrics are meant to sound anti-royal. If you listen to the recording, as I have done since 77, I suppose it is meant to create the impression that it is a symbolic two-fingered salute (one-fingered salute in the states) to royalty and the establishment.

Look more closely at the lyrics and you will see that the so-called anti-establishment song is not really an anti-establishment song at all. It's how you look at it, or should I say how you have been conned into the way you look at it that matters.

What does "God Save the Queen - the fascist regime",

symbolically and subconsciously, really mean? How many times have the followers of the Sex Pistols heard these words? How many times have they sung them?

Please read the lyrics thoroughly and ask yourself just exactly what impression has been left on the subconscious minds of those people that have heard it or sang along with it.

"God Save the Queen… we mean it *man*"

The pop music industry is completely controlled and exploited by the Serpent Cult who uses popular and talented artists to spread subliminal messages and hypnotic triggers. I believe the Sex Pistols are no different to anybody else who is exploited by the music business.

Those punks, and others, in the 1970's who thought they were being rebellious were also being duped into subconsciously supporting the Queen at her Jubilee in my opinion. Oh yes I can see the song was consciously made to look anti-royal but subconsciously it acts like any other ode to the Queen. It bloody well praises her.

'God save the Queen' was a jumbled up labyrinth of subconscious trickery created by the Serpent Cult in an attempt to get anti-royals to subconsciously worship royalty during the Heb-Sed ritual and it bloody well worked as well.

"SO '*MAN*' I REALLY MEAN *GOD* SAVE THE QUEEN SHE AIN'T NO HUMAN BEING."

In this case God is the Serpent and the Serpent represents reptilian alien beings. I told all this to the aging punk rocker who thought he had been anti- royal for decades. He was gob-smacked and mentioned the term 'the great rock and roll swindle' to me. He had to admit that the lyrics to 'God Save The Queen' were very ambiguous. Indeed if you really read the lyrics you will see that they are very *truthful* but in no way are they really anti-royal. You are just led to consciously think they are. Indeed the lyrics of the sex pistols version of God Save the Queen are a very accurate description of the Queen and those that support her.

I asked the aging punk rocker how many times he had uttered the words God Save the Queen in the 29 years since the record was released. He couldn't answer but admitted it was a million times more than any pro-royalist must have done.

Saying, and more importantly hearing, the term God Save the Queen means exactly that, you are chanting, praying, that a force saves the

Queen and it does not matter if the term *fascist regime* is used at the same time. Spiritually the act of hearing and repeating such terms, especially during rituals, increases the collective spiritual power we give away to the Serpent Cult.

Cover for the single version of God Save the Queen by the Sex Pistols. Was it really an anti-establishment song or just another form of respect?

For instance if we say 'God save Hitler - the goody two shoes regime' the term is still praising Hitler despite the reference to his regime. The same scenario applies to God save the Queen - the fascist regime. You still praise the Queen despite reference to a fascist regime. Do you get the picture now?

It is manipulation of our *subconscious*. The manipulators get you to say or hear things that are opposite to how you *consciously* perceive and react to them. It is your subconscious energy that is being deceived. Your subconscious just passes the deception onto you on a conscious level and you then innocently physically respond to that deception whilst totally believing your actions are based on truth.

The Serpent Cult harnesses such energy and it is used to keep them in power and spiritually enslave us. It does not really matter, on a conscious level, if you sing God Save the Queen and wave flags at the Queen totally in awe of her or if you are sat in a pub listening to the Sex Pistols version of God Save the Queen on the jukebox, thinking she was a waste of tax payers' money. Spiritually and subconsciously we were **all** worshipping her and endorsing her anyway. The Serpent Cult controls your subconscious so therefore you will innocently do what the Serpent Cult wants you to do on a conscious level.

It is the 'collective human **sub**conscious' that is being controlled. You cannot consciously see it or hear it and that's what makes it so difficult to expose. It is like trying to show you a piece of the wind.

The collective human subconscious is controlled by using many methods. It does not matter if the methods of control are passed on to you by the Archbishop of Canterbury or the Sex Pistols. They are both subconsciously telling you that God saves the Queen.

No matter which ocean the fish are swimming in they will all get netted.

I hope I have made sense to you on that point. The human race needs to learn how and why these things, such as symbolically praising royalty, matter. We can then start to realise why the Serpent Cult spend so much time and effort deceiving us into doing these things in the first place.

I suppose I better start mentioning my out of body experience? I am sorry to keep you waiting, as I was saying, around the time of the jubilee I had a strange out of body experience. I have only partial memory of this event so please bare with me.

I seemed to wake up in the early hours one morning in the summer of 1977. I could see myself on the bed and I felt totally weird. I seemed to be able to float through solid objects. I also felt super fit and healthy. I suddenly got the urge to float out of the window. Bloody weird I know but that is how it was. I was living in a block of flats, 4 floors up, at the time. It was dark but not too dark and dawn didn't seem too far off.

I magically floated out of the window and felt like I had the strength of a thousand men. I floated upwards, way above the block of flats and I sort of scanned the sky with my hand above my eyes, like a sailor does in the movies. The term that springs to mind is Land Ahoy! I felt like I was in a *salute* pose kind of thing, if you know what I mean. Similar to a stance you would take if the Sun was blinding you. I felt like I was trying to see, or pinpoint, something in the far distance.

I spotted a small bright light in the distance and straight away I went into a horizontal position and literally zoomed at a very fast speed towards the bright light. I was there in a matter of seconds, in an instant. I then found myself stood at the opening of a small hole on a hill. I looked around and I realised I was in the countryside around the area of Todmorden which is a small town in West Yorkshire. My home town of Burnley shares the Yorkshire / Lancashire border with Todmorden. Yorkshire is symbolised by the colour white and the rose flower and Lancashire is symbolised by the colour red and the rose flower.

I got the urge to enter the hole in the hill feet first. Once inside the hole a great space opened up. I could easily stand up inside the hill and I followed what seemed to be a narrow natural corridor in the rock. I seemed to be on *auto pilot*. I could hear voices as I approached an area that appeared to be brightly lit. I then saw three men but they appeared to be surrounded by a light haze. This haze was about 4 inches wide. I looked down at my legs I had the same 4 inch beam or haze of light around me. We all seemed to look near naked or dressed in skin coloured body stockings.

I could barely make out any of the three men's faces because they appeared incomplete. Their facial images seemed very hazy, blurred if you like, but they were obviously very pleased to see me and I somehow knew instinctively, no matter how daft it sounds, that this meeting had been planned before I was born. They all smiled broadly. I could see this through the haze and it made me feel very glad. I was very glad.

"We have waited a long time brother" one said. I nodded in agreement.

I felt an immediate bond to these men and it was very strong. We got in a small circle and all put our arms over each others shoulders. We seemed to discuss things and make plans for the future and we vowed that the next time we met would be in the flesh so to speak.

We discussed something about being betrayed and deceived a long time ago and we vowed not to let it happen again. I remember one of the men saying "I will wake you brother". One of the other men told him the same and then the third man said the same thing to him. It felt a bit like a scene from the movie about the four musketeers. 'One for all and all for one'. We held our right arms out, with a clenched fist, and all of us crossed arms like the four musketeers would cross their swords. We all started to leave the cave. We were all stood on the hill and said our farewell to each other, and we all literally zoomed of in different directions. North, East, South and West sort of thing. I felt saddened that I had left the men but knew I would meet up with them one day.

In a fraction of a second I was floating in the sky over Burnley town centre. My eye caught the sight of the union jack flag flying over the town hall which was near my home. I zoomed down, obviously out of body, and literally flew straight through the flag. The moment I did that I was back in my body on my bed. Morning had broken.

I know that experience may sound weird to most people, me included! I quickly put it down to being just a silly dream and totally forgot about it.

Two years later when I was 20 years old, after a night out with friends, I was walking home when a strange feeling came over me and my thoughts were altered immediately. I had been drinking but I was not sloshed. I was walking past the town hall steps when I noticed all the flower boxes that were laid out on the small perimeter walls. A very strange feeling came over me I suddenly ran towards all the flower boxes and tipped them over without thinking about it or worrying about the consequences of my actions. I was like a crazed idiot. There was soil and flowers all over the place and all over the steps. I came to my senses and thought for a moment, 'what the fucking hell are you doing'. I then panicked and quickly ran off hoping I hadn't been seen.

Later on something came over me again, I felt possessed in some way. After drinking further with some chums, I returned to the town hall. I then literally started climbing the town hall walls trying to get on the roof. Fortunately for me some scaffolding had recently been erected on some parts of the building and thankfully that made my strange mission easier to complete. The Town Hall was pretty high (about 50 feet at least) but I still managed to get onto the roof. It would have been impossible without the help of the scaffolding though.

I literally danced on the town hall roof, just like I was taking part in a ritual. I felt like a Red Indian doing a rain dance and I was laughing out loud. I grabbed hold of the flag that was swaying in the breeze on the flag pole. The feeling was one of total elation as I grabbed it. Made it Ma! Made it Lady in the Shirley Bassey dress!

I was really enjoying myself. Then reality hit me. I looked over the edge of the roof and saw a police car and a police van. Policemen were running around everywhere and shouting up to me.

"Get down here now you silly bugger" someone in uniform shouted at me. I started laughing to myself but more out of fear that anything else. This certainly wasn't an out of body experience but at that time I really wanted it to be! I felt like Jimmy Cagney in the film White Heat. Have you seen it? Made it Ma - Top of the world! Only I wasn't on top of the world, was I Ma?
I was stuck on top of the town hall with the police after me.

I was swinging on the flag pole. I looked down again at all the police. I realised that the few drinking mates that had been urging me on as I climbed up the building had ran off at the sight of the police. I was now on my own. Reality hit me hard and I realised again I was not on top of the world.

I was in deep shit.

The police told me to come down and promised me they would not do anything if I did. (Liars!)

I started to make my way down but it was a lot harder to get down than it was to come up. Also the spiritual power, and support, that helped me get up there had now left me. I felt deserted. I managed to make my way to the civic balcony of the town hall. I realised that this balcony was used by high ranking council figures to make public speeches. This was not to be for me though as I never got the opportunity to give a public speech if I had known what was coming I would have made a public announcement about police brutality. The large balcony doors opened and within a flash and I was pounced on and wrestled to the ground by three burly coppers and immediately arrested. I was dragged down through the corridors of the town hall and flung into the back of a police van.

I suppose actions speak louder than words!

I didn't know at that time what spiritual forces directed me to scale the domed building, grab the flag or violently overturn the flower boxes at the steps leading to the entrance of the town hall. I do know that I was severely punished for it by fives sense reality forces. I suppose my inability to explain my actions at the time led to this punishment. I really had no idea, on a conscious level, what made me do these things in my, wet behind the ears, younger days. I knew instantly though, when I had problems with the local council in 1999, that the events of twenty years earlier was not just a silly escapade by a half drunken young man after all. It was a spiritual symbolic act.

I know with hindsight that back in the 1970's, before my awakening, that I was best able to carry out this symbolic act and take the punishment as a young man. It would have been much harder for me to carry it out after my awakening in 1999 and reaching the age of 40.

Town Hall: Burnley-My Mount Everest.

....

Chapter 6
The Flag of the Sun of the Gods?

"Whistling tunes we hid in the dunes by the seaside-
Whistling tunes we're kissing baboons in the jungle"

The lyrics are taken from the song 'Games without frontiers' by Peter Gabriel

Let's get back on the path to Dendera. I have previously mentioned in this book that around 1995 / 1996 a psychic told me that I would visit Egypt in the future. I then went through what I can only describe as a fast track spiritual awakening in 1998 / 1999. The psychic mentioned many things that have since come true.

On the 5th July 2005 I approached Dendera Temple. It was 125 degrees Fahrenheit. It was what we call in Northern England, 'Bloody Boiling'. I have fair hair and blue eyes so all you gingers and blondes out there know what I am talking about. Sweaty crack is only the half of it I can tell you.

I was in a group of about twenty people and we were being escorted by an *Egyptologist* who was doing his best to tell us the official version of the history of the Temple of Hathor. Quite a few of the group had gone down with a dose of Pharaoh's revenge (the runs) and they dared not travel more than fifty yards from the sanctuary of a clean flushable toilet. They had not made it on this trip!

There had also been *terrorist* threats all over Egypt during the time I was there. Indeed bombs had recently gone off in Cairo and later on, in the Red Sea area. Guess what was the biggest fear voiced by our group in Egypt? You would think it would have been bin-Laden or some crazed Muslim militants, especially with the constant reference to them on TV, wouldn't you? But no, not in a million years! Osama bin-Laden or terrorists never entered their heads. The biggest fear by far, in our group anyway, was getting the dreaded two bob bits (the shits). Some people had a carry bag full of medicine and other potions to stop them getting the trots. They still got them though.

Having fifty pounds worth of 'stop the shits medication' from high street chemists stuck away in their luggage didn't matter in the slightest. If the Pharaoh wanted revenge he usually got it and expensive medications had no effect whatsoever. I was no exception as I was also struck by the revenge of Pharaoh', the shits, whilst in Luxor a few days later. Yuk.

I got to speak to quite a few Egyptians in the three weeks I spent in Egypt and most of them thought the 9/11 terror attack was not carried out by bin Laden or any Muslim terrorists. They thought Arabs were being made into scapegoats in a sinister frame up. I totally agreed with them.

Anyway, the first thing that took my attention at Dendera was a painting on the ceiling. It was of the goddess Nut showing her giving birth to the Sun. I don't want to drone on about Egyptian gods again and even the so-called ancient Egyptian experts don't have a clue what they are talking about and I am certainly no official expert. I am only relaying information that I felt spiritually guided to and I simply want to link modern times with ancient times and the fact that serpent and sun symbolism has always been around and it is being covertly used today, whatever way you want to interpret it. Please follow your intuition.

Here is a picture of part of the painted ceiling in the Temple of Hathor at Dendera. I was drawn to a particular place inside the temple. I was literally forcibly led to it like someone was pushing me towards it. It felt like my eyes were being forced to look at certain areas of the ceiling. .

Nun giving birth to the Sun as depicted on the ceiling at the Temple of Hathor at Dendera

This shows the birth of the Sun by the goddess Nut (personification of the sky or heavens). It is clear in the picture that you can see the feet of Nut in the bottom right hand corner. You cannot see that Nut is arched over on the picture. The picture symbolise that the cycle of the Sun is controlled by the heavens, personified by Nut. This drawing below will explain how Nut is positioned symbolising the sky or heavens.

Illustration reproduced with kind permission from Ottar Vendel

Can you now understand more easily that the Sun is coming out of the vagina of Nut?

Nut (the heavens) is giving birth to the Sun and in turn the Sun is shining on and illuminating Hathor. Nut is also swallowing the moon.

Hathor is, symbolically, the goddess of rebirth. The Serpent Cult is obsessed with symbolism and rebirth. All the ancient Egyptian temples are adorned with huge amounts of symbolism. The temple at Dendera was built to honour the re-birth of the sun god through symbolism that is dedicated to Hathor.

It is obvious to me that special rituals took place at the Temple of

Hathor at the time of the Egyptian New Year. What I would like to point out in this chapter is how Sun / Hathor rebirth symbolism displayed in the Temple of Hathor at Dendera is still being used today right under our noses.

Take a closer look at Nut (the heavens) in the picture below giving birth to the Sun from the side view.

Nut giving birth to the Sun rotated 90 degrees.

Now look a bit closer.

Close up of the painting. Can you see the stars and stripes?

That looks, to me anyway, just like the Stars and Strips flag of the USA. Do you feel the same? The same symbolism is being used in the modern day flag of the USA as it was used in ancient Egypt. Why is this? I believe that the entire American public, indeed the whole world, has been lied to about the origin of the most famous flag in the world, in modern historic terms. Ask yourself why this would happen? It is obvious that the powers that be, agents for the Serpent, do not want you to know the true symbolism behind the emblems they use, plus they need your spiritual agreement to use them.

George Washington, a 33 degree mason, arranged for the stars and stripes, also known as 'Old Glory', to be acknowledged as the official emblem of the United States of America. Here is the official version of the history of the American flag.

History of the American Flag

According to popular legend, the first American flag was made by Betsy Ross, a Philadelphia seamstress who was acquainted with George Washington, leader of the Continental Army, and other influential Philadelphians. In May 1776, so the story goes, General Washington and two representatives from the Continental Congress visited Ross at her upholstery shop and showed her a rough design of the flag. Although Washington initially favoured using a star with six points, Ross advocated for a five-pointed star, which could be cut with just one quick snip of the scissors, and the gentlemen were won over.

Unfortunately, historians have never been able to verify this charming version of events, although it is known that Ross made flags for the navy of Pennsylvania. The story of Washington's visit to the flag maker became popular about the time of the country's first centennial, after William Canby, a grandson of Ross, told about her role in shaping U.S. history in a speech given at the Philadelphia Historical Society in March 1870.

What is known is that the first unofficial national flag, called the Grand Union Flag or the Continental Colours, was raised at the behest of General Washington near his headquarters outside Boston, Mass., on Jan. 1, 1776. The flag had 13 alternating red and white horizontal stripes and the British Union Flag (a predecessor of the Union Jack) in the canton. Another early flag had a rattlesnake and the motto "Don't Tread on Me."

The first official national flag, also known as the Stars and Stripes, was approved by the Continental Congress on June 14, 1777. The blue canton contained 13 stars, representing the original 13 colonies, but the layout varied. Although nobody knows for sure who designed the flag, it may have been Continental Congress member Francis Hopkinson.

After Vermont and Kentucky were admitted to the Union in 1791 and 1792, respectively, two more stars and two more stripes were added in 1795. This 15-star, 15-stripe flag was the "star-spangled banner" that inspired lawyer Francis Scott Key to write the poem that later became the U.S. national anthem.

In 1818, after five more states had gained admittance, Congress passed legislation fixing the number of stripes at 13 and requiring that the number of stars equal the number of states. The last new star, bringing the total to 50, was added on July 4, 1960, after Hawaii became a state. (source wikipedia)

Here is a picture of the Grand Union flag.

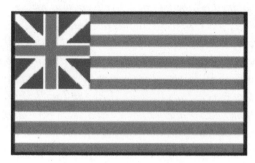

The Grand Union flag.

Please note that the flag is basically the Knight Templar cross and some suns rays stuck on it. Does this symbolise the grand *union* of the old world of ancient Egypt and the new world of the USA?

Mind you until the Grand Union flag and the Stars and Stripes flag were officially used in America and colonies and militias used many different flags. Some are famous, such as the *Rattlesnake* flag used by the Navy, with its venomous challenge, 'Don't Tread on Me'. Here is a picture of it. Please remember this image for reference later on in this book.

The Navy Rattlesnake flag

Another naval flag, known as the "Liberty Tree" showed a green pine tree on a white background. Now, where did we read about tree symbolism before?

The 'Liberty Tree' flag

It is obvious to me that the use of this symbolism was rife when the original formation of the USA was taking place. It is also plain to me that the symbolism being used at the time was linked to ancient symbolism that was displayed in Egypt. George Washington was the figurehead of the time and he was used by the Serpent Cult to ensure that the proper symbolism was used and officially adopted by the citizens of the United States. Many humans beings died while George Washington and other puppets carried out esoteric games for the Serpent Cult, using symbolism from the ancient Near East and the ancient Middle East.

It is obvious that by displaying this symbolism that it paid great dividends to those that know its meaning and use it. Maybe that's why the knowledge surrounding such things is kept behind the closed doors of secret societies. Knowledge of the symbolism was taken from the holy lands by the Knight Templar (alien agents of that time) and the same information was eventually used by Washington to lay the foundations for the growth of the USA.

Mind you, over two hundred years later George W Bush is doing the exact same thing but in reverse. This time he uses the USA flag (sun rebirth) symbolism whilst laying foundations for a New World Order in the Middle East. The flag was also used in the symbolic toppling of Saddam Hussain. I have mentioned this in my new book *'Is It Me For A Moment?'* I have also mentioned it in a free article called 'Indiana Jones and the Temple of Moab'.
You will obviously be wiser about what I am trying to say, about the symbolic use of the American flag, in that article after reading this book.

Saddam had previously claimed in public that he was the reincarnation of King Nebuchadnezzar of Babylon and he had built a full scale model of Babylon near Baghdad that was later symbolically destroyed when the coalition forces invaded Iraq.

Many people have been butchered whilst George W Bush plays silly symbolic games for his string pullers. Saddam played along with this whether he consciously knew it or not. Indeed *symbolically* the King of Babylon is currently on trial in Iraq and not some despot called Saddam Hussein. It's all an act for the Serpent Cult to carry out more symbolic ritual and perform the trickery that allows them to spiritually reign over a blind and pathetic human race.

Indeed my own personal opinion is that it is not even the *real* Saddam in the dock on trial. Why the beard? Maybe it is one of his doubles or a look-a-like actor. That said the bloke they keep pretending to put on trial does not even look like Saddam. It's just that the mass media has flashed the bearded version of Saddam in the press and on TV so often since the capture that all of us have been convinced that it is really him but he is now wearing a beard. I believe it is all a continuous game of deception. Alien agents on Earth create the deceptive situations and the masses are led along with it.

The masses simply fail to see the spiritual deceptions and clever trickery that is going.

I believe George Bush's string pullers are alien beings and their agents on Earth have been given status, power and influence and have been placed in positions of authority. They purposely arrange and carry out such symbolic events simply because alien beings want these rituals to go ahead. By allowing the rituals to go ahead it somehow gives them the right to rule over us.

The American citizens have been lied to for centuries by President George Washington and all other presidents through to George W Bush today. These secret society members have deceived their own people to carry out the will of multi-dimensional alien beings. They act as agents for a very deceptive force. The same scenario applies to all major countries in the world. England, or should I say the City of London, is the H.Q of all Serpent Cult activity. London is the Serpent's control centre in this world.

I know that is hard to take in and I will be laughed at for saying these things, but I'd rather be laughed at than you not hear this information at all. Please carry out your own research first and you will see that the symbolism being used is just too much of a coincidence. Next time you see George Bush or Tony Blair on TV look them in the eye and listen to what they say and how they say it.

See what your intuition tells you?

Mind you I'd rather be laughed at for saying that Serpent Cult secretly rules this world than actually admit I believe a word of what

George Bush or Tony Blair actually says. They have lied about everything. Everything.

Politics? *Different* political parties? Vote for the party that suits you? Bollocks. Total bollocks, a fairytale to make it look like you have a choice. You have no choice at all and even your *soul* has been 'clamped' and the political party that suits you only says the things that suit you when it is in opposition to the government of the time. The party that suits you will change colours as soon as it becomes the government. There is really only one politician party and that is the Serpent Cult party. You will never see its face in number 10 Downing Street or in the Whitehouse but it's puppet agent will always be there, at least until something is done. **It is time to wake up.**

. . . .

Chapter Seven
A Picture That Paints a Thousand Serpents

"I know you've deceived me, now here's a surprise
I know that you have 'cause there's magic in my eyes"

The lyrics are taken from the song "I can see for miles" by The Who

I would like to show you a picture of a painting that appeared in the Sun newspaper (UK). The Sun claimed the picture was painted by the hand of the late Sarah Payne. Sarah was a beautiful little girl who disappeared whilst out playing in the summer of 2000. Her body was recovered a few days later and a man, Roy Whiting, was later convicted for carrying out Sarah's murder. Sarah was just 8 years old.

The pain caused by this awful crime must have had a traumatic effect on Sarah's parents, Sara and Mike. Being a parent myself I can barely cope with even the slightest thought of this sort of thing happening to one of my own son's. Whoever committed the murder of this innocent little girl had absolutely no human feelings inside them whatsoever. No concern or pity for little Sarah was shown as they took her life without mercy. They also had no conscience regarding the drastic effect this had on Sarah's family and all those who knew and loved her.

Sarah's mother, Sara, has been used by the News of the World newspaper in recent years as a figurehead for campaigns to change laws. The News of the World newspaper, owed by Rupert Murdock, is the sister paper of the Sun. I personally believe that the same forces which caused the death of Sarah are actually behind the campaign to bring in anti-freedom laws. The fact that they use a grieving mother to assist in doing this only adds insult to injury in my opinion.

Anyway here is the picture that Sarah was supposed to have painted very shortly before her death.

The painting that appeared in the Sun newspaper on the 5th July 200, it is attributed to Sarah Payne

The painting was placed in the *Sun* newspaper and sent around the world on 5th July 2000. Sarah attended the Bell Farm Junior School in Walton-on-Thames. The picture, according to the *Sun* was on the wall in Sarah's classroom before, during and after her murder took place.

Please study the picture very, very, carefully. Sarah's mother claimed it was Sarah's painting of the kitchen in her home but this explanation does not add up.

I first saw this picture on the 5th July 2000 whilst I was on holiday with my family in Benidorm on the Costa Blanca, Spain. I bought the newspaper because I couldn't find anything else in English on sale at the time. A strange feeling came over me when I saw this painting. I knew it meant something spiritual. I obviously recognised the Masonic connections near enough straight away, because I had been studying Freemasonry throughout the previous year. I couldn't believe my eyes when I looked at all the symbolism contained in the painting.

The figure in Sarah's painting.

For those that do not understand Masonic symbolism I would like to point out that the figure in the painting is obviously a man (stubble) wearing an apron with one sleeve or one sleeve rolled up. Freemasons wear aprons during ritual and mess around with their sleeves. The apron has 33 dots or small circles on it. There are 33 degrees in Freemasonry and degrees are symbolised by a small circle. The black and white chequered floor is the usual decorative pattern used on the floor in most Masonic lodges or sun temples around the globe.

Typical chequered floor at the sun temple.

There are mainly two pillars used in Freemasonry, called Jachin and Boaz. There are also two pillars in Sarah's painting and in the painting the pillars have the name Sarah written on them.

Please note that the 'S' on the painting strongly resembles a Serpent (enlarged below). Indeed in the top half of Sarah's painting there seems to be many images of snakes. If you download the picture, it is available on Ellis Taylor's web site mentioned later, and zoom in you will find that the painting contains some very fine details and is very well constructed. Take a look at the Serpent from the painting.

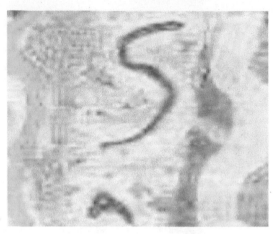

S for Sarah or S for Serpent?

Indeed please make mental note of this S image for comparison purposes later on in this book. I believe the naked man in the apron is a Mason and I also believe he is holding a Masonic ceremonial trowel. I believe that Sarah was subjected to abuse inside a sun or serpent temple and she painted what she had previously seen before her death *or* the picture was fabricated by persons unknown to make sure that the painting contained Serpent Cult symbolism to be displayed in the Sun newspaper. (Official announcement by the <u>Sun</u>) The latter could mean that further details have been added to Sarah's original painting or Sarah never painted it at all. I personally believe that Sara's painting no matter who painted it, is announcing the ritual death of a Sun Princess and that a symbolic newspaper, The Sun, made the official announcement. The similarities between Sarah's picture and Freemasonry are there for all to see. Fair enough if you cannot or won't see the symbolism but it is there for all those who can and want to see it. It is time to wake up!

I have examined the picture in very close up detail and I seriously doubt that Sarah was responsible for painting all the details in the picture. It is possible that Sarah was spiritually guided to paint the picture to somehow show the world that a ritual was involved in the build up to her death. After considering that the 'Sun' seems to be the only newspaper to have published the painting I am of the opinion that the painting is some sort of covert announcement. That announcement may have been organised by someone close to Rupert Murdoch.

Let me point out that I am in no way criticising Mrs Payne for her links to Murdoch's newspapers. I fully accept and understand that Mrs Payne is doing what she feels is right. I also encourage readers of this book to study the conclusions of Ellis Taylor at www.ellisctaylor.com regarding Sarah Payne's picture and subsequent murder.

As I have previously said I believe Sarah's mum, Sara, is being exploited by Rupert Murdoch and his media empire. I believe Sarah was selected for a sacrificial ritual by sun and serpent worshippers. Sarah was killed by agents serving multidimensional alien beings who have covertly ruled this world for thousands of years and when a sacrificial ritual takes place the Serpent Cult covertly announce such things through symbolic means, like *The Sun* newspaper.

Sarah's name was a vital symbolic part of such a ritual. **'Sara'** the mother and 'Sarah' the daughter **Ra** is Sun (god) in ancient Egypt. **Sa Ra** is known as the son, or descendant, of Ra, just like in the name CleopatRA.

SA RA

"Son of Ra" - *along with "King of upper and lower Egypt" - were the name prefixes of many of the pharaohs. The hieroglyphic signs for Son of Ra is a goose and the sun disc, giving the letters* **SA** *and* **RA**. *Note that the direction in which you read can vary - look for the direction, in which persons or animals look. They indicate from which direction a text is to be read: In this case the*

Sarah Payne has a very symbolic name she was literally named as a
sun god "princess" because she was daughter to "Sa Ra" (Royal blood
line symbolically) Sadly this symbolism alone is a good enough reason for
the bastards that carry out such things and serve the Serpent, to murder
little children. The name Sarah literally means princess.

SARAH

Means "lady" or "princess" in Hebrew. This was the name of
the wife of Abraham in the Old Testament. She became the
mother of Isaac at the age of 90. Her name was originally שָׂרַי
(Saray), but God changed it (see Genesis 17:15).

In my opinion, eight year old Sarah Payne was literally sacrificed by
Serpent Cult agents and it was literally announced in the Sun newspaper.
Using symbolism through names is for some reason, very, very important
to sun god worshippers. I am sure Rupert Murdock knew that Sarah's
picture is full of Masonic symbolism linked to ancient Egypt.

Have a look at a page from the News of the World newspaper (sister
to the Sun newspaper) in 2004. Again I want to make it perfectly **clear**
that I believe Sara Payne has no idea that she is being used by the Serpent
Cult agent, Rupert Murdoch, to announce symbolic announcements. The
editorial staff at the News of the World and the Sun will also have no
idea what is going on ritualistically or for that matter what is going on
spiritually.

Article from the News of the World newspaper

Take note of the first sentence, in bold type, of the 'serialization' of Sara's book from the news of the world newspaper.

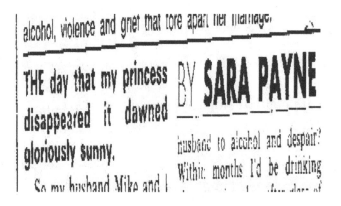

"The day that my princess disappeared it dawned gloriously sunny"

The newspaper article claims the serialisation of her book is 'entirely' in the words of Sara herself. I ask you if the quotation sounds like the words used by a normal working class woman. I suggest the words sound more like a symbolic statement than the words of a grieving mother. Are we so blind or uncaring that the painting, placed in the Sun newspaper and read by millions of people, never raised any questions within the circus of mass media?

If one of my children had been murdered and they showed me this painting and printed it in the paper I would have raised many questions. I would have kicked and screamed and shouted *what the hell is going on here.*

What would you have done?

I am also absolutely gob-smacked that this painting was not examined by child psychologists or other people with knowledge of ritual abuse. Maybe it was eh? It appears we robotically go along with life not even noticing what is actually going on right under our noses. I think it is time we moved on from Sara's story but I am sure that her painting will live inside you for future reference. Let us hope that the painting actually acts as a double edged sword and one day reveals who really was responsible for her death.

We never seem to look upwards and we blindly follow what we are told from the authorities whilst looking at the ground. We robotically do as we are told. I am sure that when we were led into the school assemble hall as children and given a hymn book containing songs and prayers that actually insulted us we would still robotically sing along with the songs and chant prayers without even thinking about it. Sadly I can think of many grown ups who would do the same thing.

Just for an example, the hymn 'Onward Christian Soldiers' could become 'Onward Stupid Sheeple and it wouldn't matter a jot to us because we would robotically sing it out loud on the orders of the school masters.

No, we are not that stupid I hear you say?

OK…Let's take a look at the true reasons behind school hall assembly in your childhood then shall we? Let's look at the Lord's Prayer for starters. Just who are we praising in the Lord's Prayer? "God" of course, I hear you say. "Which one" I ask you? The father of Jesus I hear you say? "Do we really" I reply, now laughing like a crazy professor?

I would like to remind you of the Sex Pistols song *God Save The Queen* that I mentioned in chapter five. I tried to explain how pop music can be manipulated to implant information into your mind that means something totally different to you on your everyday five sense conscious level than it does on a subconscious level. The song makes you consciously believe that the lyrics are anti-royal but subconsciously the song makes you believe spiritually that they are not.

On a subconscious level singing along with the lyrics, or simply just thinking them creates a pro-royal subconscious energy, and it is this energy that feeds multidimensional entities. It is this subconscious energy that is manipulated by the Serpent Cult and not your conscious energy. The Serpent Cult doesn't give a monkey's toss about your conscious energy, your everyday life so to speak, they control your subconscious and because of this your five sense life will just fall into place and follow suit.

The ambiguous, *God Save the Queen*, lyrics scenario also applies to religious prayer. The simplest way to explain this is by mentioning the last word used in the last sentence of the Lord's Prayer, and all other prayers come to that, that word is **Amen.**

Just what does the word *Amen* really mean? Were you, like me, told Amen meant 'so be it' and that is why you were literally forced to say *Amen* after each prayer at school? If so you were told lies like I was and you just said *Amen* like the rest of the sheep, simply because you were told to.

We really did just repeated the word without thinking, didn't we? We just wanted to get assembly over with. I went to a church school and I have lost count of the many official rituals I carried out or spiritual promises that I was forced to make to the local vicar because of them. So just what were we chanting at the end of each prayer?

Amen is an Egyptian sun god better known as Amen Ra. Now then! He wasn't Jesus' dad was he?

So, just as in the Sex Pistols song, start looking at the jumbled up information that has gone/is going directly into you on a subconscious level and try to sort it out on a conscious level. It is difficult at first but once you work it out it gets far easier. Here are the words to the Lords Prayer and I wish to use as a simple example.

The King James Bible (1611)

Our father which art in heauen, hallowed be thy name.

Thy kingdome come. Thy will be done, in earth, as it is in heauen.

Giue vs this day our daily bread.

And forgiue vs our debts, as we forgiue our debters.

And lead vs not into temptation, but deliuer vs from euill: For thine is the kingdome, and the power, and the glory, for euer,

Amen.

The final sentence really does sum the trickery up.

> **"For thine is the kingdome, and the power, and the glory, for euer, Amen."**

How many times have you uttered the words above or something very similar? Have you ever really thought what you are saying? Have you buggery! You have just robotically rhymed those words off haven't you? So has everybody else so don't worry about it. Millions and millions of schoolchildren repeat the same words day after day in school assembly halls especially in the western world. Well don't they? You are led to believe that you are just saying Amen, at the end of the Lord's Prayer, to signify "so be it". OK? Try looking at it this way for once.

> *"For thine is the kingdome, and the power, and the glory, for euer,* **Uncle George."**

Or try looking at it like this.

> *"For thine is the kingdome, and the power, and the glory, for euer,* ***Auntie Doreen"***

If you cannot see it yet, try looking at it this way.

> **"Amen,** *for thine is the kingdome, and the power, and the glory, for euer."*

Do you get it now? You are not saying "so be it" to show your agreement to Jesus' dad in heaven and to tell him he's a jolly good chap. You are spiritually stating that **Amen** has the power over you for ever and ever. You have/we have surrendered our spiritual power to *Amen*. It is as simple as that, you are taking/have taken part in a spiritual surrender ritual.

You are praising God yes, but its not the god you think you are praising. The man with the white beard who sent Jesus to save us does not really exist and you are being duped into worshipping **Amen Ra**, the sun god. You literally *give him*, for want of better words, your spiritual energy. This is because our spiritual energy can somehow be given away and a spiritual ruler can be put into power and rule over us spiritually, but only as long as we spiritually agree with it. We don't have to consciously agree with it we just need to subconsciously agree with it. It does not matter if we have been subconsciously duped into doing it either. For example, if millions of people are subconsciously made to praise "**Amen**" as our glorious power in heaven then **Amen** actually becomes our glorious spiritual power in heaven, and for ever.

"For thine is the kingdome, and the power, and the glory, for euer
Amen. *"*

We subconsciously allow alien beings to rules our lives on Earth because we unknowingly chant for them to do so. It does not matter that we have been duped into consciously chanting the names of these deities to rule over us. For example if you chant the name Everton as your favourite football team you are an Everton supporter. If you were unknowingly conned into chanting Everton as your favourite team because you thought you were really chanting for Liverpool it is still Everton that receive your support.

It's that simple.

We simply collectively vote Amen Ra into power and subconsciously accept that Amen is really a good god who has our best interest at heart. What the masses think they get-they get.

It's also on a par with consciously voting Bush or Blair into power or for that matter any other corrupt politician on a five sense level. You were duped into believing you were doing right or you were simply too blind to see what was going on.

The vast majority of us are literally forced to worship the sun god **Amen** in the guise that we are worshipping some Christian god and the father of Jesus.

This con trick is played on us when we are innocent children; easily duped innocent lambs. Our parents suffered the same fate and ironically blindly carry on the same tradition. That is why in the eye of the authorities, the biggest sin committed by the pupils of any school is to not turn up to be educated in the first place. It's a massive crime not to attend school. The authorities don't care if you fail all your exams as long as you turn up to be brainwashed in the first place. The same thing applies in all countries all over the world.

It has been pointed out to me that certain areas or certain schools in the USA don't recite the Lord's Prayer by law but they are made to swear allegiance to the Stars & Stripes flag instead. I have already given you a strong indication as to the true symbolism surrounding the origin of the US flag. It is sun god symbolism and it dates back to at least the Temple of Hathor in ancient Egypt. Swearing allegiance to this flag, and it is obviously done in good faith, is exactly the same symbolic act as giving your spirit away to Ra. It is swearing a spiritual oath that most people willingly carry out, totally oblivious to the real symbolic and spiritual meaning for doing so. It really is a fraudulent con trick in which you surrender your spiritual power. Again it is just the same principle as reciting the Lord's Prayer in that you are also respecting the Sun.

The innocent participant hasn't a clue that they are doing and to add insult to injury anyone refusing to carry out such an act will be chastised. Indeed if anyone actually questions the integrity of the symbolism hidden in the flag, they will automatically be deemed evil and immediately made into an outcast.

I tell you the truth without fear when I say that the US flag is really sun symbolism and when you swear allegiance to this flag you are swearing allegiance to the Sun. The same scenario applies to the flag in the UK and other countries.

All school pupils are conned into subconsciously worshipping Amen Ra and then all pupils are brainwashed regarding the true history and true purpose of mankind. We are taught that we are mere mortals and we should bow down to the ruling elite that are running this world.

Ask yourself why, we in the western world at least, are using the term **Amen** in the first place? What connection do we have to Amen Ra the Egyptian sun deity? I will bloody well tell you, **none whatsoever**. The only connection is that the Serpent Cult wants to enforce ancient Egyptian sun god worship symbolism on to us and they do it through trickery. We are subconsciously ordered to worship Amen but we are consciously told we are worshipping Jesus and his pop.

Why is this?

I believe a Serpent race of multidimensional beings, through their agents on Earth, need to get the masses to spiritually surrender themselves. This happens to us from a very early age and is vital for them to be able to have the control over us as early as possible and to ensure that we constantly repeat our surrender rituals throughout our entire life.

We are taught that a man called Jesus died on the cross and we should praise his father (God) for sending him to planet Earth to die for our sins. How can we refuse to go along with a sad tale like that eh? Your emotions won't let you will they? So we gladly go along with prayers as a sort of thank you to the Jesus scenario. What else can we do after he went to all that trouble for us? The same story applies to other versions of creation and other religions, the common factor being that we all accept and praise, through ritual, a Supreme Being. That Supreme Being is Amen, better known as Amen-Ra.

The major rule of Freemasonry is that you "believe in a Supreme Being" but it does not matter which one. The reason for that is that all supreme beings in this world are linked to Amen Ra. You literally cannot believe in a Supreme Being without it actually being, or at least representing, Amen-Ra. The Christian Supreme Being is Amen and so is the Muslim version. That is why the Freemasons only ask that members believe in a Supreme Being because they hold all the cards and they know all religions really represent Amen. Not that the members of these religions have the slightest knowledge of such things.

We are also all taught that if we get down on our knees and put our hands together and pray then not only do we get a god to help us but we can thank him at the same time. The action of saying prayers is deemed religious by most people but it is really just symbolism that is indicating that the human collective consciousness can literally create goodness in the world by collectively *thinking* goodness into the world. Praying symbolises that whatever the masses "think" will come to pass.

We don't need to get on our individual knees with our hands together or anything like that to make things happen. We just need to collectively think of something and it will eventually happen. Whatever it may be!

The sad thing is that the Serpent Cult created different religions to prevent this from happening. They created the *get on your knees and worship* rule no matter what religion you followed and at the same time made sure that the different religions all unknowingly worship the same sun god whilst appearing to worship a different god. Therefore we end up giving all our collective spiritual power to Amen through the symbolic act of praying (thinking) instead of collectively thinking freely for ourselves and literally creating a paradise on Earth.

Mohammed and Jesus Christ etc were stories created to cause division and hatred and not to create a loving brotherhood of man. Muslims and Christians are made to appear enemies on a fabricated battle field but then they are conned into worshipping the **same god** in the Church or Mosque without even knowing it. The blood that flows in Iraq at this time is not caused by Muslim against Christian or visa versa. It is caused by deception and trickery. Amen Ra is unknowingly worshipped by both religions but the members of each religion can't see this.

Indeed Islam has also adopted the word Amen. It has covertly appeared in their religious practises. Other mainstream religions are also duped into worshipping Amen Ra.

Here is a short extract from freemind.org website.

> *Most of us who have had the privilege of attending a Friday congregation would immediately realize the importance of the word "Amen" or "Aameen" in the life of a traditional Muslim. For those of us who are not familiar with its usage, the Muslims are required to say "Amen" after reciting Surah al-Fatihah and after*

completion of their prayers (Dua). In fact, this is the only word spoken aloud during a Friday congregation by the traditional Muslims after the Imam completes the recitation of Surah al-Fatihah

To the sceptic, who may argue against the connection between the Egyptian god "Amen" and this word used in its present day meaning, I quote the ending paragraph under the heading "Amen" from the Catholic Encyclopedia, Vol 1 1907, which either intentionally or unintentionally acknowledges this link

"Finally, we may note that the word Amen occurs not infrequently in early Christian inscriptions, and that it was often introduced into anathemas and Gnostic spells. Moreover, as the Greek letters which form Amen according to their numerical values total 99 (alpha=1, mu=40, epsilon=8, nu=50), this number often appears in inscriptions, especially of Egyptian origin, and a sort of magical efficacy seems to have been attributed to this symbol. It should be mentioned that the word Amen is still employed in the ritual both of Jews and Mohammedans." (Islam)

The entire bloody world has been conned into worshipping Amen Ra, the greatest deceiver.

Is it so strange to suggest that our subconscious energies can be hijacked and abused? Is it so difficult to accept that a small band of knowledgeable people can control all the wealth on Earth and the same people serve alien beings? This group of agents completely control the money and politics on Earth simply because of the massive power of their string pullers who are operating on a higher level of consciousness.

Do they have this power simply because we have given them conscious power over us and because we have also surrendered our collective subconscious energy to them?

Are they capable of carrying out sacrificial ritual where and whenever they want, ranging from an individual like Sarah Payne to thousands of victims in the twin towers of the WTC?

Can this group of agents and their masters create a situation where millions of lambs and cattle are slaughtered by fabricating a foot and mouth epidemic? This happened in the UK a few years back. Millions of lambs were ritually slaughtered without any proper questions being asked.

Can this group of agents create a situation where countries are invaded because of blatant lies that result in thousands of lives being lost, including women and children being blown to bits? Have agents for multidimensional forces been placed in positions of power just to enable them to carry out esoteric rituals that in turn allow their string pullers to remain in spiritual control of this planet?

These things have already happened in our world, sadly without the masses having the slightest clue what is going on, so the answer as far as I am concerned is **yes**.

. . . .

Chapter 8
We're Gonna Rock Down to Electric Avenue and Then We'll Take It higher?

"I'm going back soon,
Home to get the Baboon.
Who cut up my eye,
Tore up my Levis."

The lyrics are taken from the song 'Dr Jimmy' by The Who

Let's get back to Dendera. A strange feeling came over me in the first Hypostyle Hall in the Temple of Hathor (there are two). The word *Hypostyle* simply means that the ceiling is held up by pillars. Our guide had found a vacant corner in the hall to go through his usual tourist routine and our all the members of our group were standing around listening, or pretending to listen, to his lecture.

I had an 8mm video camera with me. I was trying to take a few indiscriminate shots inside the temple. My camera is not the best format available these days. Indeed it looked prehistoric compared to some of the cameras that other members of the group were in possession of. My camera had a very small viewfinder and it was in black and white and nowhere near the standard of some colour screens on some modern digital cameras around today. I hope you feel sorry for me about this!

As I have previously mentioned it was very, very, hot and I was not really taking any notice of the official guide. There were several other groups coming in and out of the temple and you could hear the different languages in the background. German, French etc. Suddenly a strange feeling came over me. The sound of people in the background seemed to disappear. There was utter silence. It was exactly the same strange feeling that I have experienced several times during my life.

I experienced one of these weird events when I was a young boy in the 1960's. That time the background noise faded away and all I could hear was the song playing on the radio. I mention this in my article 'Singing Do Wah Diddy'.

For a few moments the atmosphere at Dendera was just the same as it was in my back room back in Lancashire in the 1960's. I seemed to go on auto pilot. I walked, guided if you like, to another part of the

Hypostyle Hall; I had to ask myself if it was really me for a moment or had I been possessed in some way.

I automatically turned on my camera and pointed it upwards towards the ceiling as though some force was directing my arms. The ceiling in the Hypostyle Hall was approximately thirty feet high. I could see hieroglyphics on the ceiling but not very clearly. I looked through my viewfinder on the camera and had the urge to zoom in on a certain areas of the ceiling. I still couldn't see clearly. This was because of a combination of the small black and white viewfinder, my awful eyesight and the overbearing heat.

The stifling heat was causing me to sweat so much that my forehead was sopping wet and streams of perspiration were running down my face, steaming up the viewfinder lens. The area round my eye was literally sticking to the camera because of the humidity. Anyway I zoomed in and blindly took footage of a small area of the ceiling. I didn't have a clue what I was filming.

Once I had done this the background noise immediately returned to normal. I turned the camera off, job done I thought. I looked round just in time to see my group moving on to another area of the temple. I quickly rejoined the group feeling a bit embarrassed because the guide gave me sarcastic dirty look for appearing to have left the group. "You will get thirty minutes free time to look round the temple shortly" he said raising his eyebrows in my direction. That one sentence from the guide was the most informative sentence he had uttered to me all week. I knew that thirty minutes was nowhere near long enough to look round the Temple of Hathor.

I somehow knew that I was spiritually receiving subconscious 'triggers'. I was not being educated in the sense that the official Egyptologist, or the guide books, were teaching me Egyptian history. I was spiritually being shown things that were meant to trigger things off inside me, things that I already knew subconsciously but something was preventing me from gaining access to the information.

I didn't know what footage I had taken at the time, on 5th July 2005, but here are a few stills from my video camera. I am sorry about the quality but please remember these images were originally taken by a video camera being panned, blindly, across a dirty crumbling ceiling that was well over 2000 years old.

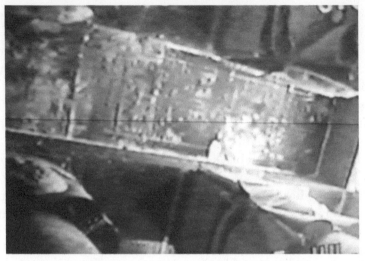

The ceiling of the Hypostyle Hall at Dendera where I blindly scanned the ceiling with an 8mm video camera- I felt under spiritual guidance

Here are some images from the ceiling. They didn't show you these in your history lesson at school, did they?

Serpent symbolism displayed on the ceiling at the Temple of Hathor

Serpent symbolism displayed on the ceiling at the Temple of Hathor.

Serpent symbolism on the ceiling at the Temple of Hathor including an
ape/reptilian being.

Please note the Ureaus, the sacred serpent, on the Kings head.

All Hypostyle Hall photos© Matthew Delooze

I have been unable to get an *official* version of the meaning of the hieroglyphs, not that the official version would mean anything to me anyway.

I would now like to draw your attention to the crypt at the Temple of Hathor at Dendera temple. I went down into the crypt through a small hole in the floor. I only had twenty five minutes to look round the large temple before the coach was leaving to return us to Luxor and the comfort of our accommodation. The air was very stale and it felt very claustrophobic. The public are not allowed access to all the crypts in the temple.

Again a weird feeling suddenly came over me but at the time I just put it down to the heat and the awful atmosphere in the crypt. I began to stare at the bas-reliefs on the crypt walls and I immediately went into some sort of trance. The next thing I remember is a fellow member of the group shaking me and saying "Come on its time to go".

A bas-relief simply means a sculpture in which the figures project slightly from the background. Here are some pictures of the bas-relief's in the crypt at Dendera. I would like to express my eternal gratitude to Larry Orcutt for allowing me to use the pictures (catchpenny.org).

The light-bulbs made famous by Erich Van Daniken at Dendera

The light-bulbs from a different angle

Is that a light bulb filament or a serpent?

Please feel free to do your own research regarding these bas-reliefs at Dendera. I will tell you that they are know as the Dendera light bulbs. Erich Van Daniken the famous author of *Chariots of the Gods,* claims the Dendera bas-reliefs are proof of the existence of ancient electric light bulbs. Although I greatly admire Mr Daniken for giving the world interesting alternatives to the rubbish we are taught in our schools, I don't believe for one minute that these images have anything to do with light bulbs.

I need to remind you about chapter 3 in this book, 'The Lotus Flower'.

Don't forget about all the stuff I told you in chapter 3 about the Sun rising out of the Sesen and order out of chaos etc. 'The creation of life by the serpents from the watery chaos' etc. I wasn't doing it for the good of my health!

A 'bigger picture' showing the light bulbs

You can see clearly that the lotus flower is featured in this image, on the left. I would like to give my interpretation of the symbolism displayed in the crypt. Please remember that the temple was built to celebrate *rebirth* or *resurrection*. Just exactly what is symbolically born through the lotus flower in these bas-relief images?

It is obviously a Serpent.

Unless you think it is an energy saving light bulb of course! The Serpent appears to be in a 'blob'. What the bloody hell is the blob?

I believe the blob is symbolism to represent the heavens or represents another dimension. The thing in the picture below supporting the blob is called the Djed

The Djed

There are many interpretations and explanations for the Djed. Here is an explanation from the altreligion.com website

>*"The **Djed** is a very ancient Egyptian symbol of stability. It resembles a short pillar with four horizontal, stacked platforms on top. It is a symbolic representation of the tree that entombed the god Osiris at his death by his brother's hand.*
>
>*The Djed was central in a festival in his honour called "the Raising of the Djed." The Djed also represented the phallus of the god, and represented the cosmic axis, or Tree of Life. The Djed can also be viewed as a representation of the human spinal cord."*

I believe that the Djed does symbolise the tree of life. I also understand the reference to the human spinal cord. The bas-relief does symbolise to me that the tree of life supports the Serpent in the heavens or the tree of life supports the Serpent in another dimension. It also indicates that the Serpent controls the tree of life.

Human figures that support the 'blob'.

The other figures under the "blob" also symbolise worship; the raising of two arms indicate this. There are also two figures on their knees in a submissive pose. This pose shows how all people in the world are at some time forced to submit their spiritual power to the heavens through the guise of modern day prayer, as mentioned in the previous chapter, be you Christian, Jew or Muslim.

Please also note and study the being holding the knives. The creature has an ape (baboon) type of body and what appears to be a reptilian head. It is very similar to the picture that I took on the Hypostyle Hall ceiling that was carrying jars.

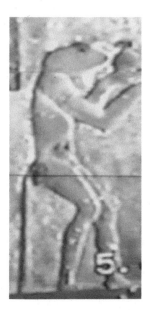

Reptilian headed apes or symbolic agents for the Serpent Cult?

I believe these images are symbolic of blood rituals being carried out by Serpent Cult agents in this world or in this dimension. The ape body represents man and the reptilian head represents the Serpent who has control of the ape (man). A reptilian dressed as a man if you like. In my opinion this symbolically represents blood ritual involving serpent and sun worship and it is being carried out by alien agents operating on planet Earth, in our world so to speak. These blood rituals are carried out to appease the covert rulers of this world. Those rulers are multidimensional reptilian beings that are alien to this world.

Sarah Payne and her painting comes also comes to my mind after seeing these images. How about you?

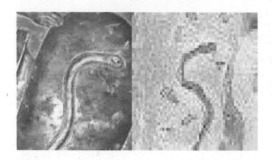

Serpents in a blob? Is it the innocent painting of Sarah Payne or a symbolic announcement from the *Sun* via Rupert Murdoch that is linked to ancient temples of the Sun?

Is the ape bodied, reptilian headed being holding knives aloft or is it holding Masonic trowels aloft?

Masonic trowels or just knives?

I leave you to come to your own conclusions. I am not trying to lead you in anyway. Maybe Mr Van Daniken is correct and the bas-reliefs really do represent ancient light bulbs? Maybe the official version is correct, but I must say I am struggling to find the official version anywhere. The British Museum has failed to provide any official answers despite several polite requests. Maybe the picture of the being on the ceiling, holding the jars, means absolutely bugger all? One thing is for sure though, you didn't get shown these things in your school books did you?

These bas-reliefs, hidden away in the crypt at Dendera symbolise to me that we are covertly taught to worship the Serpent through their agents operating on Earth. The ancient Egyptians were taught the same thing and the images in the temples symbolise this. This way of life was brought to Egypt from ancient Sumeria, Babylonia and Assyria. This is where Serpent worship stems from. I have only used ancient Egypt as a good example because a lot of temples in Egypt are still standing.

The temple at Dendera was built to symbolise rebirth or resurrection.

Rituals took place every *New Year* it is said. What was the date of the New Year in ancient Egypt, you might ask? Please don't be thinking it is the first of January either. It is not.

Here is a brief explanation of the ancient Egyptian year from the e-museum at the Minnesota State University.

> *"The calendar system of ancient Egypt is unique to both the cosmology of the Egyptians and their religion. Unlike the modern Julian calendar system, with it's 365 days to a year, the Egyptians followed a calendar system of 360 days, with three seasons, each made up of 4 months, with thirty days in each month. The seasons of the Egyptians corresponded with the cycles of the Nile, and were known as Inundation (pronounced **akhet** which lasted from June 21st to October 21st), Emergence (pronounced **proyet** which lasted from October 21st to February 21st), and Summer (pronounced **shomu** which lasted from February 21st to June 21st).*
>
> *The beginning of the year, also called "the opening of the year", was marked by the emergence of the star Sirius, in the constellation of Canis Major. The constellation emerged roughly on June 21st., and was called "the going up of the goddess Sothis". The star was visible just before sunrise, and is still one of the brightest stars in the sky, located to the lower left of Orion and taking the form of the dogs nose in the constellation Canis Major."*

Here is some more important information, for researchers, from the crystal links website.

> *"It was up to the Egyptian priests, who attended to the calendar, to sight the first rising of Sirius. At the ancient temple of Isis-Hathor at Dendera, is a beautiful statue of Isis, located at the end of an aisle flanked by large columns. The statue was oriented to the rising of Sirius and priests would place a jewel in the goddess' forehead so that the light from the returning star would fall on the gem.*
>
> *When the Egyptian priests saw the light of Sirius upon the gem on the statue of Isis they would announce to the people that the New Year had begun.*

There is an inscription on the temple which states: "Her majesty Isis shines into the temple on New Year's Day, and she mingles her light with that of her father Ra on the horizon." Ra was the Egyptian Sun god.

According to Lockyear, in 3285 BCE Sirius had replaced Draconis as the star marker of the Summer Solstice and the beginning of the Egyptian New Year. The star was used as an orientation point especially at Thebes and became identified with Isis.

The Temple of Hathor at Dendera constructed in 700 BCE is oriented to this star through the northern opening of the central passage. On the temple wall is a zodiac square which shows the star.

This is the period of time Sirius disappears from the sky - sequenced in the myth when Isis is hiding until the birth of her son, Horus - eventually the star reappears after Horus is born - resurrection. It is time!

So it was the time of the summer solstice when the Egyptians celebrated the New Year. They celebrated the return of Dog Star *Sirius* when the Sun was at its peak in the northern hemisphere. This coincided with the start of the flooding of the Nile, the *Akhet* season.

The Dog Star Sirius appeared on the horizon around 21st June in ancient times. In modern day terms the same period is in early **July**. The exact time was measured through a ritual carried out at temple of Hathor at Dendera. A statue of Isis was kept in the crypt at Dendera and every New Year it was placed in a special location so when the sunlight shone on a jewel that had been placed in the statue, the beginning of the New Year was officially announced.

I said earlier in the book that I was at Dendera on the 5th July 2005. I was in Benidorm on the 5th July 2000 when the picture of Sarah Payne's painting appeared in the Sun newspaper. I suppose in Egypt at that specific time, with the return of Sirius rising in conjunction with the Sun. *"It dawned gloriously sunny; yes it must have been gloriously sunny".*

Sarah Payne went missing on the 1st July 2000. Her body was found 18 days later. Coincidence? I don't think so. I believe the symbolic daughter of Sa Ra was used in a sun god / Serpent sacrificial ritual. Sarah went missing at the exact time of year that symbolises the ancient Egyptian New Year and the return of Sirius, the Dog Star at Dendera.

The Live 8 concerts, the G8 summit and the London bombings all took place around the time of the ancient Egyptian New Year. Is it just a coincidence?

The jewel mentioned in the statue of Isis also makes me think of the Koh-I-Noor diamond mentioned in chapter three. Is it possible that modern day crown jewels are also used for ritual purposes? Are they symbolically put on display (replicas) to attract our spiritual attention and to give our permission to agents of the Serpent to use them? Millions of people including millions of school children are led to the tower of London to view these symbolic items every year.

Do you really think the royal family gives a monkey's toss whether you see their riches or not? I believe that the modern day royal figures are just carrying out rituals to covertly gain spiritual consent from the masses and these rituals are not only similar to the Heb-Sed (jubilee celebrations), mentioned earlier in this book, they also include human sacrifice rituals. Displaying their symbolism and their riches is only a small part of it.

Anyway, let's get back on track. I think it is now obvious that the temple of Hathor was used for resurrection and rebirth rituals. They celebrated the New Year when Sirius appeared in conjunction with the Sun. The temple was built purposely for this act. It symbolises the coming together of Isis, the daughter, with her father Ra. Here is the inscription displayed on the temple of Hathor again.

> "Her majesty Isis shines into the temple on New Year's Day, and she mingles her light with that of her father Ra on the horizon."

It is obvious to me that a New Year ritual took place in July 2000 at the temple of Hathor and I believe it was connected to the death of 8 year old Sarah Payne. It is also obvious to me that the **8** mentioned in earlier chapters, created the sun god Amen Ra to be worshipped as their agent and in my opinion as long as mankind are conned into worshipping Amen Ra they are also conned into worshipping the Serpent. We are duped into worshipping Amen Ra and their descendants through many deceptive ways. Therefore we are deceived into worshipping the Serpent through the same deceptive ways. We have been duped into doing this through the use of symbolism and trickery. Worshipping the Serpent is just as much alive today as it was in ancient times. In those days they worshipped the Serpent through their *gods* such as the Egyptian god Amen Ra, the Roman god Mercury, or the Greek god Apollo. All of these gods are agents, symbolic puppets, for the real *gods* the masses were and are forced to unknowingly worship, the Serpent gods (multidimensional entities that are alien to this world).

These Serpent gods are spirit energy that expresses itself through a physical form in the shape of reptilian beings. They are really no more powerful than you or I. They are similar to the school bully and they have convinced you on a spiritual level to fear and worship them, therefore they rule you. Only you don't fear them directly, you fear their agents and their agents' descendents. This fear is not a direct *fear*, it is indirect *fear* like *fear* of poverty, *fear* of unemployment, *fear* of ill health etc.

These days we worship the descendents, the 'Sa Ra's' if you like, of the ancient Pharaohs and the bloodline of the ancient kings of Sumeria and Assyria. In the UK we symbolically worship, amongst others, Queen Elizabeth. We symbolically adore her as a central figure and an agent for the Serpent, mostly without any conscious knowledge of it. The same thing applies to other members of the same bloodline operating in other countries. Nothing has changed in the way we directly worship them as our rulers. We sing God Save the Queen and obey the rules of her kingdom. These rules are easy.

You have to do as you are told and believe your education.

It does not matter if you are forced to live a life full of poverty and misery. As long as God saves the Queen you can go to fucking hell! Worse still you can come back here through reincarnation and go through the exact same process.

Well am I right?

In these days though we still worship the ancient representatives of the Serpent Cult indirectly through mass produced pop music and 'tagged' fashions. We worship, for example (and a good one at that) the likes of the god "Mercury" through Freddie "Mercury" and Isis through the ambiguous messages/ lyrics in songs produced by the group "Queen" (Queen Isis).

It does not really matter that Mercury is suppose to be a *Roman* god or Apollo a *Greek* god. The Serpent, the greatest deceiver, has created them all. They are all agents for the Serpent. I will explain more about this in the final chapter.

I'd like to return to the Djed pillar, propping up the Serpent in the blob in the crypt at the temple of Hathor. Some people state that the Djed is also symbolic of the human spinal cord. I suppose this is possible because it certainly looks likes a spinal cord. Some people also state that the scarab beetle (dung beetle) is symbolic of the human brain and I must admit it also certainly looks like one.

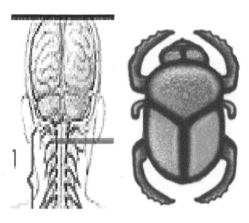

Is the Scarab Beetle symbolism linked to the two-sided human brain?

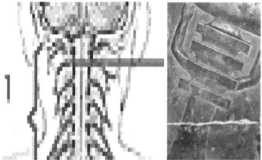

Is the Djed symbolism linked to the human spinal column?

I wish to point out that some victims of alien abduction are subjected to symbolic or physical medical operations involving the spinal column. Is it possible that one of the reasons the alien abductors carry out these operations, be they physical or symbolic, is to disconnect an individuals access to one half of their brain? It sure would explain a lot wouldn't it?

If one half of our brain stored access to spiritual knowledge, and an awareness of our spiritual intent whilst in this body on this planet, then wouldn't it be vital to anyone not wanting us to get access to it to stop us from doing so? Something on a par with cutting off the tongue of someone you didn't want to talk. That is an action that is very drastic but it is very effective. I mention in my article *"Singing Do Wah Diddy"* that alien agents on Earth have the masses under constant hypnosis and they cannot access their true spiritual awareness. Certain people are abducted because they show signs of their natural abilities breaking through that will assist them break out of the spiritual prison we have been placed in. So they are abducted and subjected to what appears to be, medical experiments or procedures to stop them from doing so.

Is it possible that the spinal cord and parts of the brain can be altered, whether in mind through hypnosis or physically through body matter, to render the individual incapable of accessing the power contained in one half of their own brain?

Has the human race been psychologically trained, physically and mentally neutered so to speak, and this has resulted in us being separated from our true power?

The bas-reliefs at Dendera certainly indicate that to me. I would like to show you a picture of the linen headwear worn by the famous Pharoah 'Tutankhamen'. I call the headwear 'Tut's cap'. Note the reference to *Amen* in the name Tut-ankh-Amen because it literally means 'living image of the lord'. In my language it means he was an agent for the Serpent. Anyway take a look at Tut's Cap.

The linen headwear worn by an agent for the Serpent. King Tut-ankh-Amen aka The living image of the Lord.

"The casing of fine linen covering the cranium of Tut-Ankh-Amen's mummy. Embroidered gold beads and semiprecious stones delineate the double uraeus,

Which indicates the scissure between the two hemispheres of the brain (Howard Carter, The Tomb of Tut-Ankh-Amon, II, PLXXXII). The single royal uraeus appears on the diadem and on the crown."

I am convinced, and have been for many years now, that negative alien abduction experiences result in the removal of spiritual awareness in people. Does this headwear indicate that the Serpent Cult is preventing mankind from assess his true spiritual powers? Is it possible that a race of inter-dimensional beings dumb us down spiritually simply to farm us? **Think about it.**

I think I have said enough for now on the Serpent in the blob, or light bulbs at Dendera. In my opinion the bas-relief images are not as enigmatic as we have been led to believe, that is if you have even seen or heard of them before. They symbolise to me that the Serpent is borne aloft by the lotus flower which is supported the by tree of life (the Djed) and the submission of mankind (the figures in submissive pose). They also symbolise that rituals have to take place to keep the Serpent in power and this is symbolised by the ape / reptilian figure carrying knives or trowels.

. . . .

Chapter 9
All the Way From Memphis.

"Forgot my six-string razor - hit the sky-
Half way to Memphis 'fore I realised"

The Lyrics are taken from the song 'All the way from Memphis'
by I. Hunter and Mott the Hoople

I was also halfway to the original Memphis in Egypt when I was in Dendera after visiting Abu Simbel, when I realised that the Serpent Cult are still using symbolic statues and other symbolism in the same way as they did in and around their temples thousands of years ago. They display statues and other monumental reminders and they are usually in places where a ritual or a festival has taken place. These monuments act as a subconscious reminder or a hypnotic trigger to us all. These subconscious reminders are connected to our *past* lives. Lives you have gone through in which you were controlled by the same hypnotic forces that still control you today in this life. In my opinion you live life after life in a vicious circle under oppressive, hypnotic control.

I need you to try and comprehend that the masses are constantly under the spell of hypnosis. Imagine a sort of wizard is at work and that he keeps the masses under a spell all of the time. The question then arises as to how the hypnotist, the wizard, keeps us all under his spell, doesn't it? Maybe the best way of understanding this is to watch a stage hypnotist and watch how the stage hypnotist keeps a small group of people under their control on *their* stage.

Please understand that most stage hypnotists only put their guests, the participants in their show, under a very mild form of hypnosis and they are not under complete mind control. The stage hypnotist, usually, only gets the volunteers to do a silly act on stage, this can vary from simply dancing around to music to taking their clothes off and shouting a few swear words etc. To get the participants to do this the hypnotist introduces 'trigger words' or 'symbolic signs' to initially set off the participant to carry out what ever the hypnotist has programmed them to do.

Triggers can be simple statements like; "When I say the words *'tomatoes on a plate'* you will prance around like an idiot". The person that has been put under hypnosis will then immediately react to the trigger words and do exactly what the hypnotist prompted them to do without thinking about it. The hypnotist had literally programmed the person subconsciously so they react consciously to the trigger words.

The hypnotist may also use signs (symbolism) and say things like, "When you *see* this '*sweeping broom*' you will take all your clothes off and dance around. When the participant sees the trigger symbolism they immediately start taking their clothes off and dance around performing a striptease act, but again, without even consciously thinking about it. I am sure you know what I mean. Hypnotism works entirely on trigger words and trigger symbolism and once you have been initially put under the spell of the hypnotist you become putty in their hands. Once the participant has been triggered the subconscious programming, primed by the hypnotist, completely takes over the participants five sense realities.

One of the best *triggers* in the world of hypnotism is music. Any sort of music can be used. The hypnotist will usually use the term "*when you hear this tune you will do this*" Obviously hypnotic music containing hypnotic lyrics acts as a double edged sword and can also be used to awaken those under hypnosis. Such has "*When you hear this tune you will not remember anything about what you have just done*". Other very good hypnotic triggers are the written word, works of art and in ancient or modern day logos.

It is very important to the hypnotist that they keep **all** their group of participants under their spell whilst on stage. If any members of the group start to come out of the spell the hypnotist will not be able to make them follow his / her trigger words and the whole act will begin to fall apart. The hypnotist is constantly watching their group of puppets and if anyone appears to be coming out of the spell they will approach them and use trigger words on the individuals that show signs of awakening to keep them under the spell. This is usually done by saying "*sleep*" and touching their shoulder at the same time or something very similar. I call this the *top-up* effect. The hypnotist 'tops-up' the awakening participant by using triggers that will increase the level that the hypnotic effect has on the individual.

If and when the hypnotism does indeed fail, the participant wakes up and they are sent back to their seat off stage, out of the way. The person that has come out of hypnosis, who has awakened so to speak, is quickly moved away from those still under hypnosis so as not to waken them also.

In my opinion this world, this five sense planet Earth is one big hypnotic act carried out on one massive stage. The same principles of the stage hypnotist still apply though. We are under the hypnotic spell of a wizard.

That wizard is the Serpent Cult. This wizard dresses up in many stage costumes and is very deceptive but the basic trickery is just exactly the same bag of tricks that is employed by the stage hypnotist you see in a club, theatre, or on TV.

Instead of using short trigger words and little signs to keep a few people hypnotised over a short period of time, the Serpent Cult use constant trigger words and constant trigger symbolism and they use them *all* of the time to keep all of the people under hypnosis. Indeed the biggest hypnotic trick of the Serpent Cult wizard is *time* itself.

Time is only as long as the wizard tells you to think it is. You only see yourself age because you were told you would see yourself age at the rate you are told to age. It is that simple but I know that is hard to take in and accept. The hypnotist wouldn't have it any other way you know!

I look in the mirror these days and think; "What the hell is going on here and why am I ageing on the outside but not ageing on the inside" I am the same boy I used to be, inside at least, so why the wrinkles and the sagging face?

It has become clear to me over the last couple of years at least, that we are collectively hypnotised into believing the three score years and ten rule. We live for approximately seventy years on average and then we die and you better believe it! How do we all get hypnotised to such an extent, without realising it I hear you say? Well for a start, when we first come into this world we are conditioned by those already living here, our parents etc, and they have already been hypnotised themselves. They are literally ready and willing, in good faith I might add, to *teach* you the true way of the world. Ironically they hypnotically teach you what was hypnotically taught to them. They have unknowingly become agents for the Serpent Cult wizard so to speak. They have become an assistant for the stage hypnotist and you are the latest volunteer participant. They, and you of course, obviously do not know this. They haven't a clue.

Once our parents have finished with us we are then *educated* by the authorities. Mass hypnosis and mind control takes place during the early years of our children's education just has the same control has taken place in our childhood. The spiritual damage done to us in our early years can sometimes never be repaired.

In ancient times everything was done through religious *scripture* both inside and outside of the temples and I have already said that the written word and pictures are very good hypnotic triggers. Hymns and prayers were also used as hypnotic tools. For example, worshipping a king or priest is not a natural instinct for a human being. The human being has to be programmed to do anything like this by a parent or a tutor and usually this indoctrination is done through fear. In modern times we have numerous media gadgets such as computers, TVs, DVD's etc, to constantly hypnotise us and leave strong triggers in our subconscious. A constant topping up of the level of the hypnosis we are all under is vital to keep the illusion, the stage act, going. The Serpent Cult will literally go to any length to keep the tops-ups going.

By the time a child reaches twelve or thirteen years old he or she has usually been hypnotically conditioned enough to officially enter the outside world that has been created for them. It is a world that contradicts their inner feelings but a world that the vast majority of people blindly go along with anyway. They don't know any different. Most of their natural intuition or spiritual awareness has been taken from them and they simply cannot access it. They cannot remember who they really are. They simply do what they have been conditioned and programmed to do.

Sometimes some people do rebel. In my opinion the spiritual energy one has, our soul for want of a better word, tries to steer the individual away from the path they are hypnotically being led down. An individual whose spirit has not been fully controlled and conditioned will rebel in someway at sometime.

Sadly this rebellious energy is usually soaked up by teenage fads and distractions of the time and these teenage fads were pre-arranged by the Serpent Cult. Teenagers seem to take solace in the fashion of their time. Teddy boys, Mods, Punk rockers, Skinheads and Goths were all created or infiltrated by the Serpent Cult to attract young souls. There is always somewhere a rebel can go and think they have escaped from the madness of their parents and the path society and authority wants to put them on. They try to separate themselves from the norm.

Let us face it who can bloody well blame them?

This separation from the norm is only for a short period though and quickly passes. Sooner or later the vast majority of teenage individuals end up back on track and follow a *norm*al life, simply because of the pressures put on them by the hypnotised masses around them and the Serpent Cult wizard of course.

The people that don't arrive back on the Serpent Cult path to a normal life usually end up in prison or some nut house to serve as an example to other teenagers who try to escape the path being carved for them. They are used to show others what happens if they start to wake up from the hypnotic path they are on. Indeed just like the stage hypnotist *outcasts* those few peopl in their group that wake up halfway through the act on stage, so the Serpent wizard also *outcasts* those that awaken from the mass hypnosis (normal life) that the masses are currently under in this world.

That is why teenagers are also targeted and conditioned by the music industry. It is vital to the Serpent Cult that when each generation comes along it is spiritually imprisoned before adulthood. The fashions and music change but the hypnotic trickery does not. It's the same trick used over and over again. The Serpent Cult just dresses it up differently to make it appear that the different generations get a *free* choice in music tastes.

I guarantee that future generations of our children will fall for the same tricks that we have done. The vast majority will be forced to follow manufactured fashion and manufactured music. Don't get me wrong I am not against music or fashion. I like music myself. I also like to party now and again! It is just that there are many, many, very talented musicians and singers out there that we never get to hear because they have not been hyped by the Serpent Cult owned music industry. The main aim of the music industry is to recruit and use selected bands to hypnotise the masses. A few subliminal messages placed in a track or two of the latest album can either make the relevant band worldwide superstars or make them massive flops.

That is why some really silly songs get to number one in the charts sometimes. It is just *hypnotism* through using subliminal messages in them. If the Serpent Cult see a song like Ernie (the fastest milk cart in the west) by Benny Hill or even the Mr Blobby song, reach number one in the charts, then they know what subliminal messages have worked the best. The hypnotised masses have actually funded the experiment as well!

I am sure you all know of a ridiculous song that's gone to number one. This is entirely due to covert hypnosis used on the masses. Hypnotised people will go running out to buy stupid songs simply because they have been triggered to do so because the songs contain subliminal messages.

Sadly along with subliminal messages, that made us buy the stupid record, there will be other subliminal messages placed in the song. Who to vote for? What to eat? Who to hate? Anything is possible when you have hypnotised the masses. They are putty in your hands. Anything is possible from causing a massive rise in the birth rate to causing a world war.

Sadly the Serpent wizard also uses hypnotised people against those people that actually manage to awaken halfway through their lives and try to raise the alarm as to what is really going on. The Serpent wizard does this by using the hypnotized people to ridicule and attack the non-hypnotised people. We literally enslave ourselves.

Just like the people under hypnosis are laughed at for their behaviour whilst performing on stage in a theatre under the power of the stage hypnotist, the opposite is true for those **not** under the control of the Serpent wizard that has hypnotised the entire world. In the case of the latter situation it is the **non-** hypnotized people who are laughed at. *Believe me I know the feeling.*

I hope that is clear. It is not easy to explain.

Anyway lets move on to the hypnotic *top-ups* that I mentioned. Like I said I believe these top-ups are used all over the bloody place. Obviously I cannot speak for the ancient world whilst in this life but I believe their hypnotic top ups were symbolic statues, scriptures or certain bas-reliefs. Cryptic scriptures were also an ideal way to get subliminal messages and hypnotic triggers into the minds of the masses and after reading such scriptures the masses did what they thought their god had told them or wanted them to do. Or should I say the masses did what the person who said they understood the scriptures told them to do. Nothing has changed really has it?

The Pope and other religious leaders claim to know what the ancient scriptures really mean so you are forced to accept their expert opinion and obey them. Those that haven't a clue what the scriptures mean just blindly follow those that claim they do. Well don't they?

Religious scriptures and *someone to worship* (religion) are the biggest and most powerful controlling techniques of them all. In ancient times they just directly worshipped the god of the day and the god of the relevant country or should I say they worshipped the relevant 'representative of God'. The Pope is a very good example but any king or any priest will do though as a further example. It did not matter that they all belonged to the Serpent Cult. They are all worshipped and obeyed for being an official representative of God.

These days we worship the ancient representatives of the Serpent Cult gods *indirectly* through mass produced pop music and fashions. For instance, we worship the likes of the god "Mercury" by worshipping Freddie "Mercury" and indeed Isis through his group "Queen" (Queen Isis). I mention this in my beside the seaside articles available free at my blog or my website.

We also worship sports stars that have sponsors that use logos that are connected to ancient symbolism. For example, the goddess *Nike* is just another rehashed version of Queen Isis. Nike was a goddess worshipped by the Greeks but all along the people were tricked into worshipping Isis instead. Just like us today the ancient Greeks and the ancient Romans were duped into worshipping gods they knew nothing about. It is all an act of trickery. For example, those people that worshipped 'Cassius Clay' in the boxing ring also ended up worshipping 'Mohammed Ali'. The changing of the *name* didn't matter. They still worshipped the same man no matter what he called himself.

Today we are bombarded with subliminal messages and surrounded by symbolism and it keeps us in a constant hypnotic trance. The symbolism just acts as a hypnotic top-up and that is why the Serpent Cult is obsessed with it.

Maybe the paragraph below will make you understand what I am trying to say on a small scale basis.

I was walking around, shopping, in the town centre the other day. It was very busy and I was getting stressed up because of the crowds. On my way back from shopping whilst carrying two heavy bags, I noticed two nuns walking towards me (a sight you don't see much of these days, I thought they had become extinct). They were dressed in their habits. I immediately, without even thinking, made extra room for them to enable them to pass me more easily. I literally surrendered to them and I automatically acted in a submissive manner towards them as soon as I saw them.

Later in the day I wondered why I had done this. Why had I shown more respect to the Nuns than I did to anyone else that was making their way through the crowds? I came to the conclusion that it was simply because of their appearance, the symbolism they were wearing, namely their habits.

I am not a Catholic, nor am I religious in anyway but that said the nuns clothing, their symbolism, made me react in the way I did. Now I ask you, how had this symbolism got into my subconscious to make me react the way I did?

On a subconscious level I was somehow forced into seeing the Catholic Church as a good and powerful organisation when I consciously know it to be a bad, corrupt and oppressive institution. It just goes to prove that subconsciously we have been hypnotised into acting in certain way when we see certain symbolism. When we see such symbolism something takes over inside us and we automatically obey the symbolism. The symbolism being used somehow overrides everything else. Just like the stage hypnotist's triggers over-ride everything else that is on stage during the show.

I believe the religious establishments of today still carry the same symbolism that they carried thousands of years ago and the masses are hypnotised into respecting it whether they really respect it on a conscious level or not. This sort of symbolism is etched into our souls so to speak because of suffering the effects of Serpent Cult hypnotic trickery lifetime after lifetime. I automatically reacted in a submissive manner towards the nuns. I have no connection to the Catholic Church at all in this life and never have had but I still reacted to the symbolism it carries!

I don't mean to say that I should have been rude to the Nuns. They were probably very nice people but just what made me react so different towards them compared to others around me? I show good manners to everyone but what made me react the way I did towards them? Have you ever experienced something similar?

Anyway back to the topping up symbolism. I believe that during our lives on Earth we are subjected to follow some kind of spiritual democratic code. I call it cosmic democracy.

I believe that the masses get just what they think they get, as you must realise by now! I call it cosmic democracy and this system of cosmic democracy only operates on our unconscious level. I always refer to the *unconscious* level as our *subconscious* level because I believe we are never actually totally **un**conscious, not even if we are in a coma.

It appears to me that our reality is created by the collective thoughts of mankind. The world is the way it is because we literally create it on a subconscious level before we experience it on a conscious level. The stage hypnotist initially puts an individual person to sleep and then plants triggers words, music or signs in the person's subconscious (unconscious). When the individual wakes up they have no idea that they have been hypnotised and they blindly follow the information the hypnotist has placed inside them, when triggered to do so.

The human race has been subjected to the same trick but on a far more massive scale and obviously the problem is actually getting people to accept this.

Do you accept it?

Can you believe you are the victim of hypnotic trickery and have been under a hypnotic spell all your life? Can you accept that this is true not only in this life but for many, many, lives before that.

No you can't really can you and I wouldn't expect you to do at this stage either. The hypnosis is very, very, strong and it is not easy to break the Serpents spell that you are under. I won't stop trying to break it for you though. Never.

You have a tiny little spark in you that knows things are not right though don't you? It is flickering away in your chest as I tell you of these things though, isn't it? I know it is because it I felt the same way a few years ago!

I have tried to feed that spark in this book. I will try and feed it a bit more in the final chapter so please follow me one last time.

....

Chapter 10
Who are you?

"I know there's a place you walked
Where love falls from the trees
My heart is like a broken cup
I only feel right on my knees

I spit out like a sewer hole
Yet still received your kiss
How can I measure up to anyone now
After such a love as this?"

The lyrics are taken from the song 'Who are you?' by The Who

Who are you? Do you know who you are? I spent 40 years of my life not knowing who I really was. Oh yes, I knew my name and I knew I was male and I knew I was a married man with two children. I knew how to laugh and I knew how to cry. I smoked, I drank and I liked a night out on the town. I like a curry. I fart and I stink just like anybody else. I have willingly and gladly spent the last twenty three years bringing up my children to the best of my ability. I thought I was a normal human being, but like you, I hadn't a clue where I came from or where I was going.

I have always felt a prisoner deep down inside myself. I have always felt controlled by the system. My experiences in childhood and some other experiences later in my life led to me to experience a traumatic spiritual awakening in the late 1990's. I realise that this kind of spiritual awakening can be seen as a mental illness or mental breakdown by people who want to see it from that point of view. If you see it that way then that's OK by me. I don't mind. If you think I am just another *loopy* conspiracy theorist, a fruit cake loony who thinks he was abducted by alien beings then that's also OK. I really don't give a monkey's because I am no longer under the hypnosis of the Serpent. I am not trying to educate you either. I don't want you to think the same as I do and I really would prefer you to think as you do and not as I do. I mean I would like you to think and speak as a free person. I would prefer to see the real you and not the manufactured clone the Serpent Cult has made you.

If you have got this far in this book, reading every chapter, then I am sure that you have questioned yourself about who you actually are too?

Welcome.

Just what forces are operating in and controlling this world you call planet Earth? What makes you the person you are? Is it the use of free spiritual intuition living a free life, or is your life controlled from start to finish by unseen faces? Consciously we all live different standards of material living but subconsciously we are all on the same level.

So…Who are you?

You, like me, are spirit energy that is *expressing* itself whilst being inside a physical body. The problem is that you are not being allowed to express yourself as you really want to express yourself.

You came in to this world to express yourself in certain ways and to experience things you simply *wanted* to experience. Things you wanted to feel emotionally, actions you wanted to carry out, anything you wanted really, be it singing in an opera to bashing bare buttocks with a bamboo cane. You came into this world to experience what you wanted to experience.

You spiritually vowed to carry out the actions that would create the situation that would lead to the experiences you wanted to happen and to help others achieve their aims too. Obviously a lot of experiences can come to pass during a typical *lifetime* and a life-plan, for want of a better word, was drawn up within you.

If you do not experience all of what you chose, vowed, to experience you will reincarnate into this world until you complete the experience and stick to your life-plan. Your spirit energy, or soul, will occupy another physical body to try and experience what you came here to originally experience.

The concept of the situation is nothing new. Several religions claim you reincarnate until you *learn* how to be good and pass the test that some god has set you and to become spiritually knowledgeable.

This religious 'coming here to learn' scenario is in my opinion, utter crap. We have not come here to *learn*, we have come here to express ourselves through our physical and emotional actions, be these actions positive or negative.

You are a multi dimensional being that can do anything you want to do when you have access to your true intuition to guide you. You chose to come into this world but now you are now trapped here and you are continuously reincarnating. You are not learning more by reincarnating you are actually having the goodness squeezed out of you lifetime after lifetime. You are not being allowed to carry out your life-plan because your natural intuition has been interfered with. You are spiritually hypnotised and have been blinded through a vicious and uncaring force.

Let me try and explain how I interpret the situation in the hope that it will help you understand and give you hope that things really are changing. I believe that we *subconsciously* create our lives, therefore create our experiences, before we *consciously* live out our physical reality. In simple terms we dream about what is going to happen to us before we actually physically experience it happening to us. We write the script, so to speak, whilst in a subconscious state and then re-enact the same script in our five sense reality or physical state.

On an individual level we may *dream* what we want to experience in our five sense reality lives only for it to come true after a short while. Many people claim to have dreamt about having a conversation with someone only for it to come true a few days later. The same can be said for someone dreaming of a domestic situation that appears to come true shortly after dreaming about it. In my opinion this sort of thing is a small glimpse of how we create our physical reality in this world, in that we think (dream) about something - it comes true - we get what we think. What the masses think they get-they get

On a collective level (all human minds working together) the same principle applies but on a majority basis. If the majority of minds in this world believe *something* then that *something* the majority believe in will eventually become our official reality.

For example the majority of people in this world believe we have landed on the moon. So in our reality we *have* landed on the moon. A few people believe we haven't landed on the moon but they are ignored simply because they are in the minority. The minority are not creating our official reality, so they are deemed mistaken or lunatics by the majority. It is only when the collective consciousness of mankind, the majority of it anyway, believes that we didn't land on the moon that our reality will change and we will demand to know why we thought we had landed on the moon in the first place. In other words; 'What the masses think they get -they get'.

We subconsciously create our reality before we consciously or physically experience our reality. We do this individually, in small groups, and collectively. Individually we subconsciously dream what we want to do in this world, like occupation, hobbies etc. Small groups (people you meet, close friends, relatives etc,) subconsciously create everyday experiences for each other, like being lovers, having children, sharing sports, etc. On a collective level we subconsciously create our physical reality of the future in global things like the weather, life-spans and historical events like landing on the moon.

For example a *small group consciousness* will subconsciously create scenarios to unfold between them on a conscious level. These scenarios will satisfy all the group's spiritual needs once they have unfolded and have been played out on a conscious five sense reality level. Whether it be having children together or having a squabble together, everybody's spiritual requirements will be met if the entire group subconsciously agree to events beforehand. The subconscious memory of having planned the scenario in the first place disappears leaving the individuals to experience a new full blown emotional event.

We planned to meet, or we will attract the people we do meet during this lifetime to help each other out spiritually. We subconsciously draw people to us who can help us experience what we want to experience.

Another example for the collective consciousness is that if all the people subconsciously wanted peace on Earth then there would be no more wars. It really is that simple.

Sadly the explanations I have given above only apply when subconscious is left to operate freely. This world, our collective subconscious if you like, has been infested with a Serpent race of multidimensional beings and they have stopped us creating the lives we want to experience.

If our subconscious thoughts are left undisturbed then we can create what we planned to experience in our five sense reality physical world and meet the persons who can help us experience what we planned to experience.

It is only when our subconscious on an individual, small group and collective levels is interfered with that our life plans, so to speak, go out of the window and the events in our lives that we wanted to experience fail to materialise.

We end up following our 'five sense material senses" which have been groomed through false state education (brainwashing) instead of following our natural spiritual intuition which is truth.

Dark alien forces lead us down the path of many turds, so watch your step.

The same forces that make us covertly worship beings that are alien to this world also arrange for the removal of your spiritual intuition or your sixth sense. That is when things turn to shit on collective and individual levels; basically we get hijacked and our individual and our group life-plans are destroyed along with a collective consciousness that would greatly improve the lives of millions of human beings on this planet, if it hadn't been hijacked by the Serpent Cult.

Our subconscious is interfered with and led astray by false education, false religious beliefs, material greed and mass media spreading subliminal messages, which in turn leads to the mass hypnosis of the human race.

There are different ways this effects people on an individual level (e.g. some will be bank robbers and some will be bigger criminals like court judges and corporate businessmen)

Obviously the vast majority of people, who have had their individual life plan destroyed, end up in mundane soulless jobs without having a clue what is going on in the world. They all end up living in total misery. This is no accident either. The loss of our full spiritual intuition leaves the individual incapable of subconsciously creating the scenarios they require to complete the events they wanted to experience. This has a knock on effect and also prevents those close to you from completing their life-plan too.

Although we are led to believe we live in a democratic free world and we can do what we like, the exact opposite is true. We are trapped in the world and for a normal person to 'get on' in the material world he or she has either to become a criminal or become totally heartless.

The collective subconscious of the human race is simply a collection of everyone's individual thoughts. All the people's thoughts (at least the vast majority) have been manipulated or forced to think in the *same* way and we are not allowed to think naturally because of the constant brainwashing spewed out by the establishment. Our ability to do so has been removed or at least our ability to think naturally is greatly reduced.

Our collective thoughts mirror how we all live, how healthy we are and even how we die. If we were allowed to live and think naturally through spiritual intuition then life on Earth would become a pleasure instead of a nightmare. If you had full access to your spiritual intuition you would create something in your subconscious (dream state) on an individual level and it would naturally come true in your physical reality. These subconscious thoughts would have been implanted in you before you were born into this world. You then wait to meet the person(s) that would trigger your subconscious into creating the scenario you had chosen to experience and visa versa, like having children, betrayal by a friend, inventing something, writing a book etc.Whatever you bloody well wanted.

I am not talking winning the bloody lottery here either. I am talking spiritual experiences that you want to feel on a physical level. You will subconsciously link up with people in and around your life and all of you will collectively create the physical reality that you all want to experience.

This is how life is meant to be in my opinion. Sadly your subconscious has been interfered with, and your plans have been sabotaged. Your mind, your subconscious, has been altered to operate on the lines that the Serpent Cult wants it to operate on and not how you want. Your spiritual intent in this world has been replaced by your material intent. Instead of following a pre arranged spiritual plan you will have been forced into a material maze of trickery instead. Dark forces have mixed up the collective consciousness of mankind.

Yes it is that simple, multidimensional alien beings have stopped the collective consciousness of the human race from operating properly. We are not capable of creating the world we really want to create or carry out the life plans we really want to follow simply because the collective consciousness that creates our reality has been infiltrated to create *their* reality. It is the classic cuckoo's nest con trick where their agenda has been placed in our minds.

In their agenda your dream state / subconscious creates material greed and covert worship of a Serpent Cult of deceivers and does not allow you reach the spiritual fulfilment that we all seek.

I would like to mention ancient scriptures for a moment, those that mention or prophesise the end of the world anyway. It is obvious that all nations wrote and left scriptures referring to the 'end times'. It is also obvious to me that life in this world was once free to experience as it was truly intended. Somehow the ancients knew and they left many prophecies stating that the world was going to suffer a catastrophic event leading to a shift in consciousness. There would come a time when people would have to make a spiritual decision or surrender to the Serpent for eternity.

Spiritual information was laid down long ago, through scriptures and symbols etc, when everyone still had access to their inner spiritual knowledge. The reason why we cannot understand the scriptures and symbols that were laid down thousands of years ago is because we had our awareness removed by a race of Serpents who had infested this world. Your spiritual knowledge has been replaced by a greedy material knowledge. Your gut instinct has been reduced to less than 3% of its true power yet your material greed and vanity has increased to immeasurable levels.

You must concede if spiritual knowledge exists along with earthy education then one must contradict the other. Not one lesson you received at school could tell you who you are could it? The limit of material education stops at the biggest bank account or the top notch on the bed post. I tell you that you are a multidimensional being with unlimited talents and not the piece of material shit this world is turning you into. You are a spiritual prisoner and once you set yourself free all your unlimited talents will return to you. I tell you this because I know it is true. I tell you this because I want to wake you up. I want you to be free again.

The ancient scriptures (albeit most of them falsely translated or purposely altered) were written in what I call one language and they only speak when you have non-hypnotised ears and eyes to hear and see them. Your state education has blinded you from even looking in the right direction.

Ancient prophecies in my opinion are just hypnotic triggers. Some were written to trigger individuals into remembering their spiritual past and some are written to keep them in spiritual slumber. The human collective consciousness put together plans to shift the mass consciousness of this world away from the dark forces that control it at present, when the time is right to do so.

I suppose the best way to describe this situation, on five sense level, is to remind you of the film 'Signs' starring Mel Gibson. If you have seen the film you will know that Mel's daughter spends all her time asking for glasses of water. Everybody thinks the little girl is daft for asking glasses of water because she just leaves then hanging around all over the house without drinking the water. It is only at the very end of the film that the reason for the girl placing the glasses of water all around the house makes sense. The little girl was acting entirely on her spiritual intuition or spiritual direction.

The little girl left the glasses of water in strategic places all around the house but nobody else understood why at the time. Just because nobody understood it did not diminish the power behind the act of leaving the glasses of water in the first place. Obviously if you haven't seen 'Signs' you don't have a clue what I am talking about, but if you have seen it you will realise that the little girls strange behaviour on a five sense level was really very powerful spiritual direction and her actions only made sense at the last minute.

The same can be said for ancient prophecies and scriptures. They won't make sense until the last minute.

Any prophecies or scriptures that attract you or me to them for study are, in my opinion, the ones we chose to study on an individual level before we were born. They are there to trigger us subconsciously when the time is right. These triggers do not happen overnight. It does not matter if these triggers are hidden in the Old Testament scriptures, native wisdom scriptures, alien abduction stories, or a book by a conspiracy theorist. They all act in the same way because they act as a key, a key to accessing the information already stored inside you. You do not need *educating* you only need the triggers that will eventually lead you to spiritual freedom. It is a key that will let you regain control of your true spiritual intuition and release you from the hypnosis you are under. Sadly for some that key can lead to traumatic experiences and it will upset some comfort zones. Some people discard or completely fail to recognise the key because of the comfort zone they are trapped in.

The past is calling for you my friend but you will need ears to hear it and to help it succeed in waking you up. There are several ways that you will be assisted in getting a pair of ears if you follow your gut instinct and not the material education you have been brainwashed with. This is because the spiritual information is already "in us". It just needs accessing. I hope I have produced a few early triggers for you. I will be a happy man if only one person gains some spiritual direction from this book.

I thank you following me through these pages. I hope that something in at least one chapter of this book sparks a few thoughts in you, be it bas-relief in the crypt at Dendera, Sarah Payne's painting, the Live 8 concerts or anything else you could connect with.

Like the girl in the *Signs* movie, I will leave my glasses of water in this book with you until they are needed, so store them where you want.

It took me forty years to realise that not only had I been lied to all my life but I had been put under very strong hypnosis, lifetime after lifetime, to keep me dancing to the tune of the Serpent.

I have stopped dancing.

. . . .

Afterword

Thank you for reading this book. I had to republish this book due to some problems I had. I am so glad to tell you that I have now written another book called Is It Me For A Moment? – Breaking The Serpent's Spell.

For those that *connected* to 'The Stars Are Falling' it is a must read book! My very best wishes go to all you truth seekers out there.

May love reign over you all.

Yours sincerely

Matthew Delooze.

List of Illustrations

Contact Details

Please feel free to contact me:

Email:

matthew@matthewdelooze.co.uk or

matthewdelooze@aol.co.uk

Website:

www.matthewdelooze.co.uk

(Under construction May 2007)

Blog:

http://matthew-delooze.blogspot.com/